Sailing *on a* Budget

Moneywise tips and deals on boat purchases, rental, dockage, destinations and more.

ANNE M. JOHNSON

BETTERWAY BOOKS
CINCINNATI, OHIO

DEDICATION

To Herb and Mary Burke
who epitomize what sailing is all about—
loving, sharing, adventuring, caring

ACKNOWLEDGMENTS

Thanks to the many sailors who eagerly shared their stories of triumph and pain over boats and the sea, and their secrets to getting things done and making them work in the least expensive way.

And to the members of the marine industry who revealed secrets, shared information and took the time to chat.

Most of all, thanks and love to my husband John, who has devoted his life to me and sailing, and who puts up with me when I am consumed with researching and writing my books.

Sailing on a Budget. Copyright © 1997 by Anne M. Johnson. Printed and bound in the United States of America. All rights reserved. No part of this book may be reproduced in any form or by any electronic or mechanical means including information storage and retrieval systems without permission in writing from the publisher, except by a reviewer, who may quote brief passages in a review. Published by Betterway Books, an imprint of F&W Publications, Inc., 1507 Dana Avenue, Cincinnati, Ohio 45207. (800) 289-0963. First edition.

Other fine Betterway Books are available from your local bookstore or direct from the publisher.

01 00 99 98 97   5 4 3 2 1

Library of Congress Cataloging-in-Publication Data

Johnson, Anne M.
    Sailing on a budget / Anne M. Johnson. — 1st ed.
        p.   cm.
    Includes index.
    ISBN 1-55870-410-8 (alk. paper)
    1. Sailing. 2. Yachts and yachting. 3. Deals. I. Title.
GV811.J627   1997
797.1'24—dc20   96-34205
                                                                                                 CIP

Interior designed by Amy Schneider
Cover designed by Brian Roeth
Cover photography by P.I. Productions/SuperStock

Betterway Books are available for sales promotions, premiums and fund-raising use. Special editions or book excerpts can also be created to specification. For details, contact the Special Sales Manager, F&W Publications, 1507 Dana Avenue, Cincinnati, Ohio 45207.

TABLE OF CONTENTS

INTRODUCTION

I remember all too well the day my husband came home excited about the news that a sailing class was forming at the navy base. Would I be interested?

I didn't hesitate for a moment—Yes. I had been on and around sailboats all my life, but never learned how to sail.

Sailing lessons were a breeze, though I never fully understood the theory. No matter how many times someone tried to explain how a boat moved through the water and the wind—"Think of it like a watermelon seed between your fingers," they cajoled—I just didn't get it. I couldn't figure out how a boat was like a seed. But that didn't stop me from sailing, or from buying my first boat, a 23-foot sloop, weeks after passing the sailing course.

There were many things I didn't understand about sailing, like reading a chart, but I learned more every time we went out on the boat. I learned I hated to heel, but loved the wind on my face, blowing my hair. I hated taking the wheel, because I still wasn't comfortable with it, but I loved traveling to a new destination by water every weekend.

And so it probably came as a surprise to my husband when, after six months on that small boat, I decided we should move aboard. He agreed, but only on a bigger boat. One year later, we owned a 40-foot Morgan Pilothouse (and crunched two households into one boat).

We joined the North Florida Cruising Club and learned about cruising and the camaraderie of the sailing fraternity. It was just a matter of time before we quit our jobs and went cruising. Since then, we have cruised all of Florida and Georgia, and a good part of the Bahamas. With each trip, we learned more and more about ourselves and about sailing. We are probably typical of most people who learn to sail and fall in love not with a sport, but with a way of life. It's not the places in our lives that have made a difference, it's the people.

To those of you who have yearned to sail, but were unsure about starting: Do it. To those concerned about living on a boat: Try it. And to those who dream of quitting their jobs, slipping the dock lines and sailing out on a lifetime of adventure: Do it now. You can always come back, buy a house and settle down again. And for the rest of your life you'll have memories of the magic of sailing.

On a more practical note, I've arranged this book to make it easy to find any particular aspect of sailing you are interested in or, if you're a novice, to help you come up to speed quickly by going through the basics first.

A handy glossary in chapter 1 provides keys to the sailing "lingo." Some of these definitions are repeated throughout the book to keep beginners from having to refer to the glossary while learning terms.

CHAPTER ONE

WELCOME TO SAILING

"The freedom of the seas is the sine qua non *of peace, equality and cooperation."*
Woodrow Wilson, 1917

"Rivers are roads which move, and which carry us whither we desire to go."
Pascal

S ailing is one of the oldest means of transportation. With three-quarters of the globe covered by water, it didn't take early man long to discover a method of transporting goods and services across rivers and oceans, not to mention discovering new worlds.

But sailing has come a long way since the days of the Phoenicians, the Vikings, Christopher Columbus and other ocean explorers, and indeed since the early cargo-carrying clipper ships graced this nation and the world. In the last five decades, sailing, and sailboats, have gone from an essential means of transportation and exploration to a sport for the wealthy to a wholesome recreation accessible and available to anyone, regardless of age, gender or physical ability.

Since the late 1960s and early 1970s, when boatbuilders began to perfect the art of mass producing easy-care fiberglass sailboats, the cost of purchasing a boat decreased dramatically, and the cost of maintaining a boat is now within the financial reach of most people.

Today, like cars, there are hundreds of makes, models and sizes of sailboats to fit every budget and lifestyle. Sailboats can be as small as seven feet long (a day sailer), or as large as forty feet or longer (traditionally called a yacht). Sailboats can even be several hundred feet long. There are entry level, mainstream and top-of-the-line models, with new boat prices ranging from $1,000 to several million dollars.

Yet, sailboats are more versatile than automobiles. Depending on size, you can put a sailboat on a trailer and drive to a neighborhood boat ramp, or tow it from city to city, state to state or cross-country. You can ship sailboats on commercial vessels and barges and transport them overseas to be sailed in foreign waters. Sailboats make great vacation homes you take on the "road," similar to a travel trailer, or they can be docked in another part of the state, or world, and used as a vacation getaway. Sailboats can serve as your home away from home, a "floating hotel" for vacations as you cruise the waterways, lakes and other bodies of water. You can sail them around the world for a trip of a lifetime. Sailboats can even serve as a primary residence. Thousands of people across the country live on boats and commute to work across a waterway, or live on a boat tied up at a marina and drive to work.

Self-contained boats that have complete living facilities and a power system to run them don't require a dock or marina. Many sailors enjoy a weekend or longer "on the hook," setting out an anchor in a beautiful, serene setting. They may take a *dinghy* (a small, usually inflatable, boat called a *tender*) along as "transportation" to get from the anchored boat to land or to explore even shallower waterways. Dinghies can be rowed or powered by a small outboard motor.

New sailboats can be custom built, partially custom built or mass produced. You can buy one partially built and finish the inside yourself, or build one yourself from scratch. Most new boats are made of fiberglass, which has proven itself a durable building material, though boats are still built from wood, steel or cement. Just about every state in the country has a boat brokerage that sells new and used boats.

There are a variety of creative ways to purchase a used boat: from a broker; private owner; insurance company when damaged; banks, credit unions and other lending institutions that have repossessed them; and from marinas when owners have abandoned them.

Like cars, boats are often financed over a short period of time, with interest rates on the loan similar to those of a new or used car. Larger and more expensive boats, those in the $25,000 and up range, are financed more like homes, with a lower interest rate and longer finance period. Interest rates on large-boat loans are usually equal to the rates of home mortgage loans. Most sailors buy their own boats, but some go in with a friend or relative and buy a boat together, splitting the purchase price, maintenance and other expenses. Some of these arrangements work well; others, well. . . .

Owning a boat may not interest you at all. If boat ownership is not in your financial or lifestyle picture, that doesn't mean you can't enjoy the sport. Rather, simply choose one of the many less expensive or less time-consuming alternatives to boat ownership: renting by the hour or day, chartering in foreign or domestic waters, crewing on racing or cruising boats, or taking care of a boat for an absent owner or friend.

For many, the first step may be learning to sail. Who hasn't wistfully watched, from land, the graceful beauty of a boat under full sail, and yearned to try her hand at the helm?

Some people think learning to sail is a complicated process. While it does require a bit of book and hands-on education, it's not as complicated as you might think. Most boating courses that provide certification for sailboat handling require eight hours of on-the-water instruction and eight hours of in-the-classroom instruction—the equivalent of one weekend. That is basic sailing. Intermediate and advanced training are available as your interest increases and your skills are honed.

Sailing is a lifelong process of learning about boats, tides, waterways, maritime rules, weather, navigation and a host of other disciplines. You don't have to learn everything at once in order to enjoy sailing. In fact, you don't have to take formal lessons, although it's a good way to learn to do things right.

And once you learn to sail a small boat, sailing a larger one is not that different. Learning to sail is no more difficult than learning to snow ski or climb mountains or white-water raft. Sailing has much in common with other sports: special equipment you must learn to use, methods for using that equipment safely and *nomenclature* (a vocabulary indigenous to the sport). In the case of sailing, the nomenclature is rich in a history that dates back to the Phoenicians. The sailing vocabulary developed from hundreds of nations speaking the same language. You'll even find that sayings commonly used in everyday speech stem from seafaring days.

But sailing offers much more than other sports. You can sail alone or with a crew. You can sail independently or as part of a group or fleet of boats. Sailing is an "equal opportunity" sport, open to everyone regardless of race, religion, gender or age. People learn to sail at age seven and age seventy; it's as easy for children to learn as it is for adults. Boats can be adapted to accommodate people with disabilities. Anyone can learn to sail, regardless of physical strength. Sailing builds confidence and self-esteem, with independence and self-sufficiency as its rewards. Sailing builds team players, too.

And sailing is truly a "green" sport that puts you close to nature. The wind supplies power without the roar of an engine, a multitude of waterways supply the highway, and your own skills and knowledge make the boat go—fast or slow.

You can find a career in sailing. Novices and pros are sought as crew on private sailboats the world over. Getting started is as simple as filling out a resume with a crew agency and being available to set sail with little notice.

The best part about sailing is that it can be done in almost any body of water throughout the United States and the world. You don't need an ocean.

There are countless lakes, bays, rivers, inlets and reservoirs in which you can sail. Some of the largest sailing clubs in the nation are in the heartland, not on the coast as you might imagine. Where you can sail is limited only by the length of the boat, its *draft* (how deep the *keel*, the lowest part of the boat, sticks down into the water), its *mast* (the pole that supports the sails) and your ability to get the boat to the body of water.

Yet, without a doubt, the best part of sailing may be the camaraderie. Unlike on land, where strangers seldom speak and neighbors don't know each other, when sailors meet they hail each other, say hello and often swap stories, share dinner or have a drink together. If you want new friends for life, take up sailing.

Sailors share traditions, customs, a language rooted in antiquity and a love for a way of life that goes beyond what the modern world can offer. To sail a boat is to share the same challenges and adventures upon the same seas that man faced hundreds of years ago. The siren of the sea is strong as John Masefield revealed in "Sea Fever":

> *I must go down to the seas again,*
> *to the lonely sea and the sky.*
> *And all I ask is a tall ship*
> *and a star to steer her by;*

But you don't have to go to sea or cross oceans to enjoy sailing. You can pick the type of sailing that best suits your lifestyle. Some people like the competition and hectic pace of racing on rivers, bays, lakes and oceans; others like the joy that comes from spending a few hours or a leisurely day on the water. Some like a combination of both racing and sailing for pleasure. Others sail to weekend destinations, using their boat as a "floating hotel." Still others take their boats "cruising" for vacations, staying away for weeks or months at a time. And a few with the dreams, money and time go on extended cruises throughout the nation and abroad. It's your pick. Do what *you* enjoy.

That said, owning a sailboat can be a costly endeavor. You've heard the adage, "A boat is a hole in the water that you throw money into." Yes and no. For many, sailing is a way of life. If you buy a boat as an investment, you'll most likely be disappointed. Put your money in the stock market instead. But if you buy a boat as a way to have access to the water, to get closer to nature, as a hobby, an adventure or a means of seeing the world, you won't be disappointed. Just be prepared for the full cost of ownership. Besides the initial purchase price, you may have to pay monthly rent to keep your boat at a marina in the water or on land, and pay the cost to haul it out of the water annually to paint the bottom. You'll have to invest in regular maintenance, which includes engines, sails and overall upkeep (like varnishing all those beautiful teak railings).

In general, the smaller the boat, the less the cost to purchase and maintain it, and the more time you'll have to spend on the water. Most boat services and dockage are charged "by the foot."

But there are tried-and-true ways to save money and still sail, regardless of boat size and the type of sailing you do. That's what this book is about—choosing a sailing lifestyle and maintaining it as inexpensively and enjoyably as possible.

 TIP

If you buy a boat with living accommodations—a kitchen and bathroom, called a *galley* and *head* respectively—under most circumstances the Internal Revenue Service allows a deduction for the interest paid on the loan because it qualifies as a "second home."

A BEGINNER'S SAILING GLOSSARY

Bow The front of a sailboat (jokingly called the "pointy" end).

Crew People who help sail and maintain a boat, or who provide a service, such as cooking, for pay or for pleasure.

Cruising Sailing done on a leisurely basis, usually for a night or more, to a destination near or far.

Galley The kitchen.

Head The bathroom.

Keel A protuberance at the bottom of the boat that stabilizes it and keeps it from sailing sideways.

Mast The tall pole (or poles) that carries the sail.

Monohull A sailboat with one hull.

Multihull A sailboat with two or more hulls; a catamaran has two hulls, and a trimaran has three.

Port The left side of the boat. Easy to remember, because port and left both have four letters.

Racing Sailing in a competitive atmosphere, usually under an organized body such as a sailing association or yacht club, often to win an award.

Sailboat A boat that uses sails as its primary means of propulsion; the boat may also have an auxiliary source of power, such as an inboard or outboard motor, or oars.

Sailing The art and science of making a boat move in the water using sails for power.

Sails Sheets of canvas or other strong materials that catch or deflect the wind and make the boat move over water.

Starboard The right side of the boat.

Stern The back, or rear, of the boat (the "blunt" end).

CHAPTER TWO

GETTING STARTED

Where you start depends on many factors, including how much exposure you've had to sailing and your experience. If you've never been on a sailboat in your life, but think it would be fun to learn, the best place to start is to get on a sailboat. While this may sound overly simple, it's not. Many people are unprepared for the boat's *heel* under sail, which is the way it leans toward one side or the other, especially on *monohulls* (sailboats with one hull). Monohulls are the most common type of sailboat. A *multihull*, like a catamaran or a trimaran (boats with two or three hulls), stays fairly level—it has very little heel. Monohull sailboats are not level when under sail and some people find this uncomfortable, even at a slight 5° to 10° heel. If heeling is enough to make you quit right then and there, don't give up: Switch to a multihull boat.

If you have been on a sailboat and think you might like to learn more about sailing, you can sail a few more times to be sure, or jump right in and start learning through friends, acquaintances or a sailing school.

If you have the basics down pat, consider an intermediate course. Once you've done that, try your hand at special-interest or advanced sailing courses. That could include learning how to cross oceans, how to cruise for long periods of time or how to race, including the tactical maneuvers and rules of the art of racing.

There are a number of inexpensive ways to learn sailing skills.

YOU'VE NEVER SAILED BEFORE

Sure, you can take costly lessons, buy a boat and *hope* you like sailing. Don't. Many people are lured to sailing by romantic notions only to find out they don't like the sport, don't have time for it or want to go faster than a sailboat is able to go (in general, about five *knots*, or a little over five miles per hour).

Before you spend money on sailing lessons, get out on the water on a sailboat and see if you enjoy it. Here are some inexpensive ways to find out if you like sailing as much as you think you will:

• Find a local sailing or yacht club and go to their meetings. Meet other sailors. Talk to them. One of them might extend an invitation for you to sail. If you don't know if your city has a sailing club, ask friends and acquaintances. Look up marinas in the phone book and ask the owners or managers if they know of any sailing clubs. Go to docks at marinas and talk to other sailors; they may know of clubs, or may invite you on board to take a look around. Sailors are a friendly lot who love nothing better than to talk about the sport. Liveaboard sailors have a name for visitors—"dock stompers," or "wanna-bees"—but nevertheless, they will often invite them aboard or at least spend a few minutes talking with them.

Call the local newspaper and talk to the boating reporter about sailing clubs. Or check at marine stores and marinas for local sailing publications: Many of them are free, and some list sailing organizations in the area.

Call sailboat brokers and talk to them.

• Take a test run. Many brokers now offer, usually at least annually, an opportunity to sail. Some tie the event in with a charity fund-raiser and charge a minimal amount, say $10 or $20, to go out for a sail. Others have a standing policy of letting prospective sailors go out for a ride; most, however, don't. It doesn't hurt to ask. Check with boat brokers or manufacturers, and watch sailing publications and newspapers for notices of such special events. Also, more and more large sailboat shows offer free sailing outings.

• Go on a half- or full-day sail on a crewed boat. If the boat is small, the skipper may allow you to try your hand at the wheel, or *tiller*, and being on the water in a sailboat for four hours or more will give you a pretty good idea of what to expect from sailing. You'll see what skills you'll need to learn and will learn something about the degree of difficulty that's involved in learning to sail.

• Take out an advertisement in your local newspaper asking for someone to teach you to sail. You might offer something in return, perhaps help with boat chores. You may be surprised at the number of responses you will receive.

• Read classified ads in boating magazines and newspapers. A few sailors earn extra money by taking novices sailing or by teaching them to sail.

I'M HOOKED, WHERE CAN I SIGN UP?

Once you've decided that sailing is a sport you think you'll enjoy, learn all you can. There are many ways to do this.

• Take formal sailing lessons. Your choices include local sailing clubs and yacht clubs, the American Red Cross, community groups, including city- and state-funded programs, sailing and racing organizations and associations, U.S.

TIP

Colleges and universities located close to bodies of water sometimes offer a variety of courses on sailing and marine skills to the public at a nominal cost. Classes may include beginning sailing, advanced sailing, marine mechanics, small engines and navigation. These courses may be less expensive than others in the area. Also, some colleges may sponsor a sailing club that owns a boat or a fleet of boats for its members' use, either free or for a nominal charge.

Navy bases (for active duty or retired military personnel and their families, plus some government workers), sailboat rental and charter companies and sailing schools. Find them through local, state or national chapters, or in the phone book. Look under Sailing, Boating, Chartering, Rentals, Marinas, Marine Facilities or combinations thereof. (The telephone numbers of national organizations and some of the largest national and a few regional sailing schools are listed at the end of this chapter.)

The American Red Cross, for example, has chapters throughout the nation. Individual chapters decide whether to offer sailing lessons, according to John Ewing of the Orlando, Florida, office. A state may have a few chapters or many; there are more than thirty chapters in Florida. Usually, a chapter covers a county or metropolitan area.

The Orlando program is led by volunteers who conduct basic (thirty-hour) and advanced (thirty-six-hour) sailing courses, two sessions a week over a four-week period. Part of the training takes place in a classroom at the Red Cross office, and the hands-on portion takes place in a nearby lake. Courses are offered every month except December and January, and are open to anyone, any age. Prerequisites include the ability to swim laps and turn a small sailboat over and set it upright again. Red Cross certification is provided upon successful completion of the course, which includes a written test.

• Sign up as crew. If you're willing to learn, many racers will teach you to sail if you agree to crew with them for the season. Although most skippers prefer crew with rudimentary skills—people who already know the basics, including the nomenclature—some will be willing to teach you. You'll find such opportunities in many of the same places listed for sailing lessons.

• Ask friends who sail to teach you. If you ask around, you may be surprised how many people in your social and work worlds sail, or know someone

TIP

Save money on sailing books. Browse through used book stores close to marinas for a wide choice. Exchange your nonsailing books for sailing ones at a marina's book exchange.

who does. A laid-back cruising sailor may be happy to have you aboard and teach you. Or you might be able to work out a deal where you agree to help maintain a boat in exchange for the owner teaching you to sail.

- Surf the Internet. There are more than fifty World Wide Web sites on the Internet that offer information on sailing. Many of these sites are web pages started by sailing enthusiasts whose goal is to provide free information and support for sailors. Use a search engine, such as Yahoo!, to find them. Online services such as America Online and CompuServe have sailing sites, as well as online sailing magazines and forums online. You also can purchase, and sometimes download as shareware, software that teaches you how to sail.

- Visit the library or a bookstore. Hundreds of books on sailing have been published over the years. You can check them out from the library, or buy them and learn at your own leisure. From the books you'll learn sail theory and, most importantly, the nomenclature, which every sport has. For instance, you'll learn that on a boat, the left side is the *port* side, the right side is *starboard*, the pointy end or front is the *bow* and the back or the rear is the *stern*. These are important terms to know because they refer to the vessel. If the skipper tells everyone to go to the port side, he means the boat's left side, not yours (which may differ depending on where you and the other crew members are sitting or standing). Magazines on sailing can be checked out of the library or purchased wherever magazines are sold in your area.

- Rent videotapes. Videotapes on sailing may be available for rent or to purchase from a library, a ship or marine store, boat manufacturers and sailboat brokers. Some rent tapes for a nominal fee, but may require a deposit. Others may simply loan you the tape. Video rental stores and libraries may also carry a small selection of tapes on sailing.

TIP

Most sailing magazines offer discount rates for new subscribers. Call the publication to find out if such rates are available.

TIP

Many sailing publications that charge a subscription rate are free when you pick them up at marinas or marine stores.

- Join a sailing club. Many local sailing clubs allow people who don't own a boat to join. Clubs may or may not have annual dues, or may charge very little to join, perhaps $10 to $40 a year. Most have monthly meetings with speakers, and allow for time before and after the meeting to meet other sailors. You're sure to strike up a conversation with someone, and most likely someone will ask you to go sailing. Also, if the club sponsors races or cruises, and most do, members may ask at meetings for people to crew with them for a particular event.

- Go to boat shows. Most states have boat shows several times a year, usually between October and March. Warm-weather states such as Florida and California have shows year-round. Boat shows can be large, such as the international boat show held each January in Annapolis, Maryland, where thousands of boats and boating exhibits can be seen, to state shows such as the one held in Miami Beach, Florida, where exhibitors and boats number in the hundreds, to local shows held in smaller cities. Some shows offer sailing demonstrations, sell videotapes, and offer free sailboat rides. Boat shows also are a good place to meet other sailors and people in the field who may lend a sympathetic ear if you tell them of your interest in sailing. They may also give you tips on who is looking for crew, or on free sailing programs coming up in your area.

- Take a basic course from a sailing school. Most sailing schools offer an inexpensive beginner's course where you'll learn the basics. The least expensive, but not necessarily the best, provide six to eight hours of classroom and text-book instruction. This is where you'll learn the names and uses of different parts of the boat, such as *winches*, devices that help you pull in or let out lines used for various purposes, and *standing rigging*, the wires that support the

TIP

Combine sailing lessons with your vacation: For the price of a week in a hotel on land, you can spend a week on a boat learning to sail.

mast. You'll also learn the *points of sail*, the directions in which a boat can sail, and *sail theory*, how the boat moves through the water using the wind. But textbook learning is no substitute for doing. If you're already sure you want to pursue learning to sail, take a course that combines classroom instruction with hands-on training on a boat in the water.

TIP

Check your state and county marine and fish commission and marine law enforcement agencies for free boating-safety courses. The Game and Fresh Water Fish Commission in Florida, for example, offers a free boating-safety course in most counties.

SAILING SCHOOLS

Although sailing schools can be found in most states, they tend to be concentrated around popular cruising and sailing destinations—the west and east coasts of the United States, including all coastal areas of Florida. You'll also find large concentrations outside the states in popular tourist destinations in the Caribbean. These can be small, privately owned schools or large schools owned by national corporations, often with branches in several states and countries. The quality of instruction, not the size of the school, is what matters.

Costs vary as well. Smaller schools may be less expensive than larger ones; schools in popular vacation destinations may charge more, because of higher demand, than schools in cold-weather cities or small towns. Other variables include the size and type of boat used, the number of people in the class and the length of the class.

For example, Tulsa Sail-Craft Co. in Tulsa, Oklahoma, only offers an occasional basic course—textbook and classwork combined with a Saturday on the water for $65—according to owner Jim Burke, because demand for sailing lessons is limited.

By contrast, Offshore Sailing School, which has two schools in Florida, two in the Caribbean and one each in New Jersey, Connecticut and Rhode Island, offers year-round instruction, except for the school in New York. The lowest tuition is $375 for a beginner's course in New York, according to Kirk Williams, vice president of marketing.

Such schools usually provide a choice of classes, starting with a beginner's course, "Sailing 101," moving to an intermediate course, which usually qualifies you to charter a boat, and then on to specialized areas such as "Blue Water (ocean) Sailing," "Liveaboard Cruising" or "Racing Techniques."

One important thing to note about sailing school certification, according to Captain Chip Winans of Sea Safari Sailing in St. Petersburg, Florida, which is devoted strictly to teaching and chartering multihulls (catamarans and trimarans, boats with two or three hulls), is that there is no one governing body for sailing certification, even though several national organizations claim to be the governing body. This is important because schools that offer certification from one of those national bodies may claim it is the only certification charter boat companies will accept for *bareboat charters* (taking the boat by yourself without the charter company's crew, which costs extra). And some may insist that you take two courses or more to earn that certification, which costs you more time and money.

The truth is, charter companies don't require special certification. They simply want to ensure that you are capable of taking a boat out by yourself and bringing it back safely. Many well-qualified sailors have never been to a sailing school, learning instead on their own boats over the years or on someone else's boat. However, if you are new to sailing and have limited experience, a charter boat company will probably not rent to you unless you can either prove your skills at its location before your take the boat out or you can provide proof that you have successfully completed an intermediate learn-to-sail course.

Sailing schools may provide their own certification, or they may provide certification from a specific sailing body, such as the American Red Cross or the American Sailing Association. Winans suggests that you see what the difference is between "101" and "202" courses; often, you will learn the same things in 202 as you do in 101. His company, for example, tries to talk students into taking the latter course. At Sea Safari, 101 is a two- to three-day class and 202 is a five- to seven-day class, but 202 covers the basics covered in 101. The cost for a two-day class is $395 for one person. All of the classes are *liveaboard*, which means students actually live on the boat on the water during class time. The rate includes instruction, lodging, food and at least an overnight cruise.

"We have a manual and a classroom on the boat, so you learn and then practice what you learn each day," says Winans. "It's productive because people learn better when they're having fun."

Sailing schools teach people of all ages, and even entire families, but most require that children under age eighteen be accompanied by a parent or adult.

You also will want to find out how many people are in a class at the school you select. Some schools cram a boat full of people even though it is more difficult to learn that way. You are apt to learn more in a smaller on-the-water class because you will have the opportunity to do more. Training can also be customized to the varying skill levels of individual students.

Don't overlook community sailing organizations. Each year, more than one thousand community sailing programs in the United States introduce 300,000 people to sailing. These programs may be operated by states or cities, or by sailors who simply love to share the sport with others. Many offer free or nominally priced lessons for a variety of levels, and some have a fleet of boats that members can use for free or for a small fee. Some have monthly meetings, speakers, cookouts, organized races and cruises and other fun outings.

You can find sailing schools in the yellow pages or in sailing magazine and newspaper advertisements. Some magazines publish an annual guide to sailing schools. Several sailing associations have toll-free numbers you can call to find a sailing school in your city or in a city close to you. The National Marine Manufacturers Association, for example, offers a "goody bag" of information to people interested in sailing. When you call its toll-free number, the association will send you a list of sailing schools in your area, a guide to community sailing programs, an easy-to-read booklet on how to sail, and a free subscription to or copies of sailing magazines.

 # TIP

Sailing schools in competitive areas continually offer discounts. These may be for off-seasons, which will vary with the area (in warmer states, off-season is the summer months; in colder states, it's winter or the rainy season), or to gain business during other slow times. Also, many schools follow up on their marketing. If you call for a brochure and don't respond within three months, chances are good that the company will mail you a discount coupon, say seven days for the price of five, or five days for the price of three. You can also try to negotiate a group rate, or a lower rate if the class is nearly full or business is slow.

I'VE GOT THE BASICS DOWN PAT. WHERE DO I GO NOW?

Once you've learned the basics, you're ready to go further, depending on where your interests lie. Most charter companies and sailing schools offer secondary and advanced courses that range from ocean sailing to navigation to long-distance cruising skills.

One of the more popular ways to learn to sail is to combine training with a vacation. By doing this, the boat becomes both your hotel and your classroom—with meals included.

Prices vary, depending on the location, type of boat, instruction, length of time out and activities planned. At Offshore Sailing School, for example, which has taught seventy-eight thousand people to sail since 1964, the price for a one-week course in a vacation area is $850 per person, double occupancy. Airfare is usually separate, but ask if the school offers a package rate or discounted airfares.

U.S. Power Squadrons across the United States offer sailing and boating courses in classrooms at community halls or public schools. The courses, taught by qualified volunteers, are usually free, but textbooks may be extra. You don't have to own a boat to sign up.

The U.S. Coast Guard Auxiliary also offers courses for a variety of skill levels. They are taught by volunteers, so the type and frequency of courses offered vary by state and by auxiliary.

And if you haven't crewed with someone yet, you're ready to offer your services now. Chapter 4 gives more in-depth advice on crewing. The biggest advantage to crewing is that you get hands-on training. You can submit a resume to a professional crew company for a job such as cook, and if you're hired you'll gain valuable ocean-sailing experience while you get paid to cook.

Or you may want to rent, charter or buy a sailboat. There's more information on each of these choices in other chapters.

TIP

Rent a house and get the use of a sailboat free. Look in the classified sections of sailing magazines and newspapers for waterfront vacation rentals. Sometimes a sailboat will be included in the cost of the house rental.

ASSOCIATIONS

American Red Cross
(703) 206-7090

Call local chapters for information on sailing programs

American Sailing Association
13922 Marquesas Way, Marina Del Rey, CA 90292, (800) 877-7774, ext. 1512

An association of sailing schools, instructors and sailors. Provides documentation of on-water experience and certification of training for sailors and instructors throughout the United States. Members receive discounts on gear, equipment, sailing lessons, charters, travel and more. Open to the public. $29 a year for an individual.

Boat/U.S. (Boat Owners of the United States)
880 S. Pickett St., Alexandria, VA 22304, (800) 245-2628

A boat owners association that provides many benefits, including free towing insurance and literature on numerous topics, plus a newsletter. Also provides the names of local sailing schools. Membership discounts available through participating sailing clubs.

BOAT/U.S. Sailing Hotline
(800) 336-BOAT

Provides information on free boating courses offered by the U.S. Coast Guard Auxiliary and the United States Power Squadron.

National Boat Owners Association
(800) 852-6262

Provides towing, free charts of your area, 25 percent discount at participating retailers, directory of stores that provide discounts and services, theft protection program and 50 percent savings on cellular phone service.

National Marine Manufacturers Association
Chicago, IL, (312) 946-6200, (800) 535-SAIL (535-7245)

"Discover Sailing" program gets you a bag of goodies and has a network of four hundred sailing schools that offer a free half-hour lesson to those who would like to try sailing for the first time.

United States Power Squadron
Raleigh, NC, (919) 821-0281

US Sailing
P.O. Box 1260, Portsmouth, RI 02871-6015, (401) 849-5200

Provides a list of U.S. schools that teach racing and has a free publication, "Where to Sail," containing detailed information on more than nine hundred community sailing programs nationwide. Publications department has other free literature available. The full text of "Where to Sail" is on CompuServe's The Sailing Forum.

SAILING SCHOOLS

(This list is a sampling.)

CANADA

Cooper Boating Center
1620 Duranleau St., Vancouver, BC V6H 3S4, Canada, (604) 687-4110

Harborside Boating Center
275 Queens Quay, W., Toronto, ON M5V 1A2, Canada, (416) 203-3000

Independence Afloat Sailing School
283 Queens Quay, W., Toronto, ON M5V 1A2, Canada, (416) 203-2299

Ontario Sailing Association
1220 Sheppard Ave., E., Willowdale, ON M2K 2X1, Canada

Specialty Yacht Sales
102-1676 Duranleau St., Vancouver, BC V6H JL4, Canada, (604) 689-7491

CARIBBEAN

Chilmark Community Center
1cd5 Winberg Park, St. Thomas, VI 00802

KATS St. John
P.O. Box 37, St. John, VI 00830

Ocean Incentives
American Yacht Harbor at Red Hook, St. Thomas, VI 00802,
(800) 344-5762

Offshore Sailing School
Treasure Isle Hotel, P.O. Box 68, Road Town, Tortola 00065,
(800) 221-4326

Regatta Time in Abaco
Marsh Harbor, Abaco, Bahamas, (809) 367-2222

Roosevelt Roads Yacht Club
MWR Dept., P.O. Box 3015, Navsta, R RDS Ceiba, PR 00735,
(809) 865-3297

St. Croix Sailing School
P.O. Box 2043, Fredriksted, St. Croix, VI 00841, (809) 772-2482

GULF STATES

Incentive Sailing Program
126 Lavergne St., New Orleans, LA 70114

Jimmy's Barter Sailing School
P.O. Box 6059, Diamondhead, MS 39525

North American Sailing School
9124 Seabright Ave., Elberta, AL 36530, (800) 635-3747

Sail Louisiana
P.O. Box 30485, New Orleans, LA 70190

MIDWEST

Action Marine
328 N. Andover Rd., Andover, KS 67002

Buck Jones Sailing Center
1101 W. Winona Ave., Warsaw, IN 46580

Carlyle Sail 'N' Surf
P.O. Box 144, Bresse, IL 62230, (618) 594-2461

Corpus Christi International School of Sailing
P.O. Box 995, Corpus Christi, TX 78403, (512) 881-8503

Dakota Sailboats
415 Third St., Devils Lake, ND 58301, (701) 662-4955

Flatland Sailboats
444 N. Cedar, Red Cloud, NE 68970, (402) 746-3314

Fox Valley Sailing School
P.O. Box 145, Menasha, WI 54952, (414) 766-8707

Geneva Lake Sailing School
524 South Shore Dr., Fontana, WI 53125, (414) 275-2727

Great Lakes Sailing School
Bldg. 160 NTC, Great Lakes, IL 60088, (708) 688-6978

Gull Lake Sailing School
5717 Drew Ave., S., Edina, MN 55410

Jack Leverenz Sailing School
1177 Cadieuz Rd., Grosse Point Park, MI 48230, (800) 521-8802

Kentucky Lake Sails
P.O. Box 129, Highway 453, Grand Rivers, KY 42045

Lake Beulah Sailing School
N8736 Wilmers Point Lane, East Troy, WI 53120

Lake Minnetonka Sailing School
P.O. Box 757, Excelsior, MN 55331, (612) 474-6708

Nicky Pleass Sailing School
4885 Woodland Dr., Sandpoint, ID 83864

North Texas Sailing School
501 Yacht Club Rd., Rockwall, TX 75087, (214) 771-2002

Pistakee Yacht Club Sailing School
252 Lippincott Lane, Fox Lake, IL 60020, (708) 587-6460

Red Rock Sailing School
Park Center #331, 500 First St., N., Newton, IA 50208, (515) 791-4625

A Sailing Affair
1702 W. Twenty-Ninth, Austin, TX 78703, (512) 476-8341

Saint Louis Sailing Center
13616 NW Industrial Circle, Bridgeton, MO 63044, (314) 298-0411

Tulsa Sail-Craft Co.
4411 S. Sheridan, Tulsa, OK 74145-1136

Wind Over Water Sailing School
1871 W. Fifth Ave., Columbus, OH 43212, (614) 488-1468

NORTHEAST
Annapolis Sailing School
P.O. Box 3334, Annapolis, MD 21403, (410) 267-7205

Big Bass Lake Sailing Program
P.O. Box 113, Gouldsboro, PA 18424, (717) 842-6388

Charlotte Sailing Center
Rt. 2, P.O. Box 2503, Converse Bay Rd., Charlotte, VT 05445,
(802) 425-4106

Chesapeake Sailing School
7074 Bembe Beach Rd., Annapolis, MD 21403, (410) 269-1594

Coastal Sailing School
11 Everett Paine Blvd., Marblehead, MA 01945, (617) 639-0553

Eastern Shore Small Craft Institute
1700 Chelmsford Circle, Newark, DE 19713, (302) 454-1700

J World
P.O. Box 1509, Newport, RI 02840, (401) 849-5492

Lake Hopatcong Sailing School
1 Mountain Shores Rd., Lake Hopatcong, NJ 07849, (201) 663-3724

The Landmark School
Prides Crossing, MA 01965

New England Sailing School
P.O. Box 323, Durham, NH 03824, (603) 868-2350

New Jersey Sailing School
P.O. Box 691, 1715 Bay Ave., Point Pleasant, NJ 08742, (908) 295-3450

Norwalk Sailing School
P.O. Box 157, Georgetown, CT 06829, (203) 852-1857

Oyster Bay Sailing School
P.O. Box 447, West End Ave., Oyster Bay, NY 11771, (516) 624-7900

Sailing School of Baltimore
1700 Bowley's Quarters Rd., Middle River, MD 21220

Salty Bill's Sailing School
8801 Shore Rd., Brooklyn, NY 11209, (718) 934-6653

Sawyer's Sailing School
254 Summer St., Auburn, ME 04210, (207) 783-6882

Sea Sense
25 Thames St., New London, CT 06320, (800) 332-1404

Sea Space Sailing Center
505 Sconticut Neck Rd., Fairhaven, MA 02719, (508) 994-3333

Twelve Islands and Beyond
5431 MacArthur Blvd., NW, Washington, DC 20016, (800) 345-8236

NORTHWEST

The Anchorage
P.O. Box 578, Lyons, CO 80540, (303) 823-6601

Corinthian Sailing
P.O. Box 4213, Olympia, WA 98501, (206) 754-6506

Four Winds
P.O. Box 140, Deer Harbor, WA 98243, (206) 378-2277

Island Sailing
2100 Carillon Point, Kirkland, WA 98033, (206) 822-2470

Portland Sailing Center
3315 NE Marine Dr., Portland, OR 97211, (503) 281-6529

Puget Sound Sailing Institute
5632 Marine View Dr., Tacahoma, WA 98422, (206) 383-1774

Quiet World Sailboats
15 E. Montana, Kalispell, MT 59901, (406) 755-7245

The Sailing Center
6101 Caufield St., Suite A, West Linn, OR 97068

San Juan Sailing
1 Harbor Esplanade, Bellingham, WA 98225, (206) 671-4300

Seattle Sailing Club
5900 W. Greenlake Way, N., Seattle, WA 98103, (206) 285-3067

PACIFIC

Haleiwa Surf Center
P.O. Box 507, Haleiwa, HI 96712, (808) 637-5051

Hickman Harbor
15 MWRSS/MWRO, 900 Hanger Ave., Hickman AFB, HI 96853, (808) 449-5215 (Military Base)

SOUTHEAST

Bahia Mar Resort and Yachting Center
801 Seabreeze Blvd., Fort Lauderdale, FL 33316, (305) 764-2233

Blackbeard Sailing School
P.O. Box 19634, Atlanta, GA 30325, (404) 351-9463

Chapman School of Seamanship
4843 SE St. Lucie Blvd., Stuart, FL 34997, (407) 283-8130
   Professional marine courses and other sailing skills

Hilton Head Sailing Center
728 Schooner Court, Hilton Head, SC 29928, (803) 671-2727

Home Port Sailing School
Rains Rd., Rt. 667, Bohannon, VA 23021, (804) 725-7424

Mariner Sailing School
P.O. Box 7093, Alexandria, VA 22307, (703) 768-0018

Martins Sailing Instruction
10910 Griffing Blvd., Miami, FL 33161, (305) 895-1050

Naples Sailing Center
896 River Point Dr., Naples, FL 33942, (813) 649-1073

Nashville Sailing Center
P.O. Box 507, Hermitage, TN 37076, (615) 883-3336

Nor'banks Sailing Center
1308 Duck Rd., Duck, NC 27949, (414) 261-4369

Offshore Sailing School
16731 McGregor Blvd., Fort Myers, FL 33908, (941) 454-1700

Oriental's School of Sailing
P.O. Box 127, Oriental, NC 28571, (919) 249-0960

Points of Sail Sailing School & Navigation
P.O. Box 5227, Destin, FL 32540, (904) 654-1518

Sail Amelia
P.O. Box 755, Fernandina Beach, FL 32034, (904) 261-9125

Sail Harbor Academy
P.O. Box 30392, Savannah, GA 31410, (912) 897-2135

Tega Cay Sailing
117 Mary Louise Court, Fort Mill, SC 29715

Treaure Harbor Marine
200 Treasure Harbor Dr., Islamorada, FL 33036, (305) 852-2458

SOUTHWEST
Adler Marine
3375 Rolling Hills Dr., Lake Havasu City, AZ 86403, (602) 855-1555

Lake Havasu Yacht Club
805 Minor Dr., Lake Havasu City, AZ 86403

Lakeside Sports
P.O. Box 129, Logan, NM 88426, (505) 487-2930

MacQueen's Marine
P.O. Box 572, Highway 196, Rt. 7, Texarkana, AR 75502

Sun Set Sailing
P.O. Box 30, Tumbling Shoals, AR 72581, (501) 362-7194

WEST COAST
Big Bear Marina
P.O. Box 130206, Big Bear Lake, CA 92315, (714) 866-3218

California Adventures
U.C. Berkeley, 2301 Bancroft Ave., Berkeley, CA 94720, (510) 642-4000

California Sailing Academy
14025 Panay Way, Marina Del Rey, CA 90292, (310) 821-3433

Club Nautique
1150 Ballena Blvd., Suite 161, Alameda, CA 90292, (510) 865-4700

Club Sail
909 Marina Village Parkway, #418, Alameda, CA 94501, (510) 522-7423

Dana Harbor Yacht Charters
34571 Golden Lantern, Dana Point, CA 92629, (714) 493-1206

Ocean Voyages
1709 Bridgeway, Sausalito, CA 94965, (415) 332-4681

COMMUNITY SAILING
(This list is a sampling.)

GULF STATES
Fair Harbor Marina
831 N. Section St., Fairhope, AL 36532, (205) 928-3417

Trail N Sail
6701 Stars and Stripes Blvd., New Orleans, LA 70126, (504) 244-9516
    Boat dealer for MacGregor, Seaward and West Wight Potter that offers free one-week sailing course in conjunction with members of South Shore Yacht Club.

MIDWEST
Alpena Community Sailing
322 State St., Alpena, MI 49707, (517) 356-4172

Community Sailing Program
225 N. Market, Suite 333, Wichita, KS 67202, (316) 267-9227

Des Moines Park and Recreation Department
3226 University Ave., Des Moines, IA 50311, (515) 237-1428

Hoofer Sailing Club
800 Langdon St., Madison, WI 53706, (608) 262-1630
    University of Wisconsin Madison: twelve-hundred-member club on Lake Mendota. Membership open to students, faculty, staff, alumni and others. Fleet of fifty boats, including sailboards. Teaches novices; provides unlimited sailing instruction.

Iowa Sailing Club at University of Iowa
(319) 644-3785, website: http://chop/isca.uiowa.edu:80/sail/hello.html
    Teaches daysailing and racing to new members for free. Has forty-five-boat fleet and facilities on Lake MacBridge. Holds three membership drives a year.

Northeast Indiana Sail Association.
P.O. Box 4001, Hammond, IN 46324, (219) 738-3086

NORTHEAST
Burlington Community Sailing Program
216 Leddy Park Rd., Burlington, VT 05401

Community Boating, Inc.
21 Embankment Rd., Boston, MA 02114, (617) 523-1038

Community sailing program where children sail for $1 a season. Programs for adults.

Courageous Sailing Center
Boston Harbor, Charlestown Navy Yard, 1 First Ave., Charlestown, MA 02129, (617) 242-3821
Teaches adults to sail. Adults "buy" a boat for the April through October season for $100. More than 140 boats in fleet; fourteen to twenty-three feet.

Croton Sailing
P.O. Box 620, Croton-On-Hudson, NY 10520, (914) 271-6868

Downtown Sailing Club
P.O. Box 39483, Baltimore, MD 21212, (301) 727-2884

Philadelphia Sailing School
P.O. Box 611, Riverside, NJ 08075, (609) 461-3992

NORTHWEST
Access to Sailing
19744 Beach Blvd., Suite 340, Huntington Beach, CA 92648, (714) 722-5371

Bellingham Yacht Club Community Sailing
2625 Harbor Loop, Bellingham, WA 98225, (206) 733-7390

Cal Sailing Club
1 Seawall Dr., Berkeley Marina, Berkeley, CA 94706
Nonprofit cooperative on San Francisco Bay dedicated to teaching sailing. Meets monthly at Berkeley Yacht Club. Offers free sailboat rides to the public one weekend a month, and monthly barbecues, also open to the public. Membership includes free sailing lessons and use of equipment. Two dozen sailboats. $45 year; students, $40.

The Center for Wooden Boats Community Sailing
1010 Valley St., Seattle, WA 98109, (206) 382-BOAT

Juneau Sailing Club
3225 Hospital Dr., Juneau, AK 99801

Ketchikan Community Sailing Foundation
P.O. Box 8973, Ketchikan, AK 99901, (907) 225-6701

Nautical Heritage Society
24532 Del Prado, Dana Point, CA 92629, (714) 661-1001

Olympic Circle Sailing Club
1 Spinnaker Way, Berkeley, CA 94710, (510) 843-4200

The Sailing Foundation, 7001 Seaview Ave., NW, Seattle, WA 98117,
(206) 784-2653

SOUTHEAST
Charleston Parks and Recreation Department
861 Riverland Dr., Charleston, SC 29412, (803) 762-2172

Coconut Grove Community Sailing
3969 Hardic Rd., Coconut Grove, FL 33133, (800) 468-4440

Norfolk Naval Sailing Association
MWR Dept., Bldg. C-9, Navsta, Norfolk, VA 23511, (804) 444-2918
(Military)

Orlando Yacht Club Community Sailing
4218 Arajo Court, Belle Isle, FL 32812

Rudder Club of Jacksonville Community Sailing
8533 Malaga Ave., Orange Park, FL 32073, (904) 264-4094

ONLINE RESOURCES
America Online
Sailing magazines, chat room and sailing forums.

CompuServe
Online Yacht Club
Sailing help, tips and information for racers and cruisers.

Sailboats Inc!
Offers $50 off its sailing classes if you register via its web site on the Internet.

SailNet World Wide Web Site
145 S. Livernois, Suite 304, Rochester, MI 48309, (810) 651-9404, E-mail:
info@sailnet.com, website: http://www.sailnet.com (918) 663-2881

MAJOR SAILBOAT SHOWS
Chicago Boat Show
(312) 946-6262

Miami International Boat Show
(305) 531-8410

National Marine Manufacturers Association
(312) 946-6262
    Provides the date and place of a boat show near you. The information is limited to shows it sponsors.

New York National Boat Show
(212) 984-7070

Philadelphia Boat Show
(610) 449-9910

SailExpo
Atlantic City, NJ, (800) 329-4386

Seattle International Boat Show
(206) 634-0911

U.S. Sailboat Show
Annapolis, MD, (410) 268-8828

SAILING MAGAZINES AND NEWSPAPERS

BOAT/U.S. Reports
880 S. Pickett St., Alexandria, VA 22304, (703) 823-9550
    Bimonthly magazine of Boat Owners Association of the United States. Free to members.

Cruising World
5 John Clarke Rd., Newport, RI 02840, (401) 847-1588
    Twelve issues, $28.

The Florida Mariner
P.O. Box 1220, Venice, FL 34284, (941) 488-9307
    Has "Boat Lovers" personal ads. Free at Florida marine stores; twenty-four issues, $39.95.

48 Degrees Latitude North Sailing Magazine
6327 Seaview, NW, Seattle, WA 98125
    Twelve issues, $15.

Heartland Boating Magazine
Inland Publications, Inc., P.O. Box 1067, Martin, TN 38237,
(901) 587-6791
    Covers lake and river sailing in mid-America. Seven issues, $16.95.

Living Aboard
141 N. Roadway, New Orleans, LA 70124, (504) 283-1312
    Trials and tribulations of living on boats. Six issues, $12.

Mid-Gulf Sailing
141 N. Roadway, New Orleans, LA 70124, (504) 283-1312
    Twelve issues, $14.50.

On Deck
6752 Gordon Rd., Suite 3, Wilmington, NC 28405, (800) 815-1088
    Twenty-six issues, $24.95

Practical Sailor
P.O. Box 420235, Palm Coast, FL 32142-0235, (800) 829-9087
    Twenty-four issues, $39.00.

SAIL Magazine
P.O. Box 10210, Des Moines, IA 50336
    Twelve issues, $23.94.

Seaworthy
BOAT/U.S. Marine Insurance and Damage Avoidance Report
880 S. Pickett St., Alexandria, VA 22304, (703) 823-9550
    Free to insured members. Four issues, $10.

Soundings: The Nation's Boating Newspaper
35 Pratt St., Essex, CT 06426, (203) 767-3200
    Twelve issues, $19.97.

SAILING VIDEOS

Bennett Marine Video
2321 Abbot Kinney Blvd., Venice, CA 90291, (800) 733-8862

SAIL Videos
By *SAIL Magazine*, (800) 362-8433

CHAPTER THREE

SPECIAL SAILING PROGRAMS

Sailing programs for special groups of people—women, children and the disabled—are becoming more common. Because sailing has traditionally been a man's sport, fewer women have learned the joy of sailing. This is changing as the number of schools dedicated to teaching women increases.

Many schools, such as Women for Sail and Womanship, are run by women for women and offer courses ranging from beginning sailing to advanced ocean sailing. These schools have chapters located throughout the United States, and in international waters as well. Some offer special rates and, in general, their rates are competitive with other sailing schools.

Lesser known are those sail programs for people with disabilities. The nonprofit group Shake-A-Leg offers sailing lessons and charters for people with a variety of disabilities. Similar groups provide boats specially equipped to meet the needs of paraplegics, people who are sight- or hearing-impaired, or who have physical or mental limitations. Most boats and equipment are donated; lessons and use of the boat are free or offered at a small cost. Some even have sailing clubs.

Other specialized programs are designed specifically for children. Boy Scouts and Girl Scouts offer summer camps with sailing programs, and some offer regular weekend programs. Local sailing clubs and yacht clubs often provide sailing lessons for children, as do some city and state recreation programs. U.S. Youth Sail Racing also offers programs for children and programs aimed at disadvantaged youth.

SAILING PROGRAMS FOR WOMEN

Women's sailing programs have proven popular for several reasons: Women learn differently than men—they often benefit more from "doing"; some husbands and fathers, having learned how to sail by making mistakes, are reluctant to allow their wives and daughters do the same, especially when the mistake may mean hitting the dock and scratching the boat; and, as anyone who has taught his or her own child to drive will acknowledge, teaching someone close to you to sail can be nerve-racking, often accompanied by yelling when mistakes are made. So widespread is this belief that the motto of one women's sailing school is "Nobody yells." Finally, until women learn to sail, they often are relegated solely to "drudge positions" (cooking, cleaning, and raising and lowering the anchor) and miss half the fun of sailing. Or worse, their only function on the boat is to follow orders on an "as needed" basis, which is also not much fun.

The worst part of this, since most cruising couples are a husband and a wife team, is that if only the man knows how to sail and something happens to him at sea, the nonsailing partner is vulnerable to a host of situations that could prove life-threatening.

Besides special sailing schools for women, a growing number of private and community sailing clubs and organizations have programs, races and cruises geared specifically to their female members.

Once women learn to sail, gender becomes less of an issue. Though some continue to participate in races and other programs specifically for women, they are also comfortable in predominantly male or gender-mixed sailing groups.

Womanship lays claim to being the first sailing school *for* women *by* women, according to owner and founder Suzanne Pogell. The Annapolis, Maryland-based company has grown from offering one course in one location with 60 students the first year (1984) to a variety of courses taught in New England, the Chesapeake, Florida, the Northwest, the British Virgin Islands, Greece, Tonga and New Zealand, for women, couples and families. The company now teaches about fifteen hundred students a year; 98 percent of them are women.

Two-, three-, five- and seven-day courses on a boat are taught to women who want to learn to sail, or who dream of being a skipper or sailing instructor. Their motto is the famous "Nobody yells." Prices range from $272 for a two-day program to $2,675 for a fifteen-day adventure overseas in Greece, Ireland, Tahiti or British Columbia. Some overseas locations change from year to year.

The company also has a special clinic, "Sail Yourself Home," aimed at women who sail with a partner but who don't know how to sail themselves.

"It's aimed at women who are terrified at the thought of having to be in charge if something happens to the skipper," says Pogell. A video and work-book with step-by-step how-to's also are available.

"We've provided a profession for women," says Pogell, in what was once a man's world. "We give them the skills, and the confidence, and time on the water to qualify."

Organizing a group of women to take a course nets the group a 10 percent discount.

Women's Sailing Adventures of Westport, Connecticut, owned by Sherry Jagerson, teaches liveaboard courses for women in New England, on the West Coast and in the British Virgin Islands. In business for six years, the instructors are all women who teach exclusively women.

"Most of the women we teach have some knowledge of sailing," says Jagerson, "but they've been taught, perhaps, by a husband or father, and along the way they've missed a lot."

In Jagerson's courses, every aspect of sailing, from anchoring to navigation to crew positions to cooking to man-overboard drills, is learned along the way by each student. Each student in the seven-day course has a crew position that changes daily, plus an additional job such as safety officer.

Students fly directly to their boat of choice in Maine, Washington's San Juan Islands, the British Virgin Islands, or elsewhere, and start to work as soon as they arrive.

A week-long liveaboard course averages $1,100 for seven days, including meals and lodging (on the boat).

For the budget-conscious, Jagerson recommends: "off-season in the Caribbean—it doesn't get any hotter in the summer"; agreeing to go on a short list—going at the last minute in the event that someone else cancels, which could mean a savings of 10 percent; or organizing a group of four or more, with a 10 percent discount for the organizer. This company seldom has introductory offers.

WOMEN'S SAILING PROGRAMS
Hurricane Island Outward Bound
P.O. Box 429, Rockland, ME 04841, (800) 341-1744

Seattle Women's Sailing Association
6202 Fifteenth Ave., NW, Suite 545, Seattle, WA 98107

Womanship
The Boathouse, 410 Severn Ave., Annapolis, MD 21403, (410) 267-6661

Women For Sail
537 Edgewater Ave., Oceanside, CA 92057, (619) 631-2868

Women Offshore
Offshore Sailing School, 16731 McGregor Blvd., Fort Myers, FL 33908,
(800) 221-4326

Women's Sailing Adventures
39A Woodside Ave., Westport, CT 06880, (800) 328-8053

SAILING PROGRAMS FOR THE DISABLED

At one time, sailing was thought to be only for the hale and hearty. The rigors
of moving about and operating a sailboat, combined with weather conditions
that can change in a moment's notice from fair and sunny to windy and wild,
were thought to make sailing an unattainable goal for people with disabilities.

But time and experience have proven those theories wrong. With boats
designed to accommodate people in wheelchairs and modern technology that
can help the deaf to "hear" and the blind to "see," disabled people are taking
to the water in greater numbers than ever before.

In fact, in 1995, the Paralympics added sailing to its competitions for the
first time, and there is now a national championship, called the Independence
Cup.

Community organizations have added programs and instruction for disabled sailors, and formal programs are springing up worldwide.

The U.S. Sailing Association has a subcommittee called Sailors With Special
Needs (SWSN) that serves as a clearinghouse and focal point for disabled
sailors, their able-bodied friends and sailing programs. It sponsors the Independence Cup.

Chairman Robie Pierce, who has multiple sclerosis, estimates the number
of formal programs for the disabled nationwide at about a dozen. They can
be found in San Diego and San Francisco, California; Seattle, Washington;
Chicago, Illinois; Boston, Massachusetts; Newport, Rhode Island; Miami and
St. Petersburg, Florida; and in the Chesapeake Bay area. New programs spring
up each year.

Most of these formal programs are run by volunteers. The two largest are
Shake-A-Leg in Miami, Florida, and Rhode Island (Pierce is director of the
latter), and the Judd Goldman Adaptive Sailing Program in Chicago.

Such programs open the world of sailing to people with physical and devel-
opmental disabilities, including mental retardation. Some programs also are
geared to those with visual and hearing impairments. Most of these programs
teach people to sail, but some simply provide access to the water for those
unable to participate in boat-handling.

Although one of the first sailing programs for the disabled, the Lake Merritt

Adapted Boating Program, began in Oakland, California, in 1981, what really opened the world of sailing to the disabled was a boat designed in 1986 by Gary Mull and built by Tillotson Pearson, Inc. The *Freedom Independence 20* was built from the keel up to accommodate people with disabilities. Harry Horgan, founder of Shake-A-Leg, a New England term that means "get up and do something," approached Tillotson Pearson about designing such a boat after he became a quadriplegic. The boat has been continually refined since then and about thirty-five are used in training programs around the country. Unsinkable, and equipped with a chair that swivels from side to side, the boat's hardware and setup make it easy for the most severely disabled to handle.

Horgan asked boat designer Mull to design a boat in which he could sail, and in 1986 the first boat was ready. Horgan's organization has grown to three facilities, the original in Rhode Island, another in Miami, Florida, and a third in San Diego, California. The Miami group is now a separate corporation, and Horgan serves as director.

Shake-A-Leg has expanded to include a variety of impaired people who learn to sail and enjoy the group's offerings, according to Miami Assistant Director Allen Fiske. Fiske, who has a spinal cord injury, realized his dream of living aboard his own boat.

Applicants must be able to perform some function, such as steering or handling a line, or to just be comfortable on a boat ride.

Shake-A-Leg teaches the disabled to sail—and to get involved. It builds communication and teamwork skills, which helps build self-esteem.

Shake-A-Leg offers a free introductory sail, and then offers basic, intermediate and advanced sailing lessons at $300 per twelve-week course. Last year, the Miami organization served two thousand people.

The organization has a sailing club that sponsors race regattas and overnight trips. For $400 a year, members have access to the fleet of six specially designed sailboats and two power boats.

The Miami group recently received a grant from the Knight Foundation for a pilot program to teach people who are vision- and hearing-impaired to sail.

SAILING PROGRAMS FOR THE DISABLED
MIDWEST
At the Helm
1500 FM 2094, Suite 3472, Kemah, TX 77565, (713) 334-4104

Great Lakes Adaptive Sailing
15114 St. Paul, Grosse Pointe, MI 48236, (313) 822-3091

Judd Goldman Adaptive Sailing Program
Chicago Park District, Marine Dept., 425 E. McFetridge Dr., Chicago, IL 60605, (312) 294-2270

Milwaukee Community Sailing Center
1450 Lincoln Memorial Dr., Milwaukee, WI 53202, (414) 277-9094

NORTHEAST
Chesapeake Region Adaptive Boating (CRAB)
1007 Beech St., Annapolis, MD 21401, (410) 974-2628

East Pier Sailing
81 Rockway, Weymouth, MA 02188, (617) 340-1129

Hoofers Accessible Sail Program
University of Wisconsin, 800 Langdon St., Madison, WI 53706, (608) 262-1630, E-mail: dziegle1@facstaff.wisc.edu

National Ocean Access Project
P.O. Box 33141, Farragut Station, Washington, DC 20033, (301) 217-9843

Sail Connecticut Access Program
65 Pilots Point Rd., Westbrook, CT 06498, (203) 453-5284

SeaLegs: The Handicapped Sailing Experience
380 Bleeker St., Suite 154, New York, NY 10014, (718) 987-6837

Shake-A-Leg
P.O. Box 1002, Newport, RI 02840, (401) 849-8898

US Sailing
Sailors With Special Needs, Robie Pierce, (401) 846-5549

US Sailing
P.O. Box 209, Newport, RI 02840, (401) 849-5200

SOUTHEAST
Sailing Alternative
4012 Plumosa Terrace, Bradenton, FL 34210, (813) 792-9698

Shake-A-Leg
2600 S. Bayshore Dr., Miami, FL 33133, (305) 858-5550

WEST COAST
Bay Area Disabled Sailors (BADS)
P.O. Box 193730, San Francisco, CA 94119-3730, (415) 281-0212

Challenged America
9625 Black Mountain Rd., Suite 207, San Diego, CA 92126-4564,
(619) 586-1199

Footloose Sailing Association
2319 N. Forty-fifth St., Suite 142, Seattle, WA 98103, (206) 528-0362

Lake Merritt Sailboat House
568 Bellevue Ave., Oakland, CA 94601, (510) 444-3807

Mission Bay Aquatic Center
1001 Santa Clara Place, San Diego, CA 92109, (619) 488-1036

Orange Coast College Sail Program
1801 W. Pacific Coast Highway, Newport Beach, CA 92663, (714) 645-9432

Santa Barbara Sailing Center
The Breakwater, Santa Barbara, CA 93109, (800) 350-9090

YOUTH SAILING PROGRAMS
Sailing programs for children and adolescents are the largest of all specialized programs. Nearly every yacht club has a youth sailing program; many community organizations and sailing clubs have regular or special summer programs. In addition, the Boy Scouts of America, the Girl Scouts of the U.S.A. and other youth-oriented groups offer sailing to junior members.

Several youth racing organizations oversee national and international competitions. US Sail Racing's program leads to Olympic trials and participation.

Though sailing schools and organizations that serve all sailors may accept children, the organizations discussed here concentrate on youth activities.

Boy and Girl Scout troops offer training to members on a troop-by-troop basis. That means becoming a member of a troop. But in some areas these councils may offer a summer camp where basic sailing is taught, and such summer camps may be open to nonscouts. Some scout councils have permanent facilities on the water where sailing is taught on a regular basis. Check with your local scouting council to find out about specific programs and offerings in your city or state. For the Girl Scouts, a call to the national office will put you in touch with someone who can find a sailing camp in your area.

Some communities have innovative programs designed for children that also include adults. The oldest and largest is Community Boating, Inc., of Boston, Massachusetts. Founded in 1941 as a way to give children access to the river basin, it has expanded, since incorporating in 1946, to provide sailing opportunities to people of all ages. Its motto is "Sailing For All," according to Executive Director Peter Lyons.

Under the program, children can receive sailing lessons and can sail as much and as often as they want on the organization's huge, varied fleet of boats for $1 per summer.

"We found we couldn't charge a dollar per kid and break even," says Lyons, "so we started adult memberships."

Community Boating now has 1,500 members ages ten through seventeen who sail for $1, and 3,300 adults who sail April through October for $100 a season.

The all-volunteer organization has a fleet of over 140 boats, which includes wind surfers, sea kayaks, Cape Cod 14s, Flying Juniors, 13-foot Lasers, 18-foot Cape Dorys and 23-foot Sonars.

These are used in a variety of programs, including beginner, intermediate and advanced sailing classes.

"Most of these are kids from the city who have never set foot on a boat before," says Lyons.

As members learn to sail, they in turn teach other members; Lyons learned to sail there when he was ten years old. That's the secret of keeping down the cost of membership, since the organization does not receive government funding. Fund-raisers also help pay the way.

Another Boston program is the Courageous Sailing Center, a ten-year-old government/business partnership run by the City of Boston's Division of Parks and Recreation on the Charles River.

This year-round program teaches an average of seven hundred urban Boston children a year, from ages eight to twenty, to sail. There is no charge and long waiting lists are common. When these junior sailors reach age fourteen, they're eligible to begin teaching others and are paired with senior instructors.

"They learn about mentoring, leadership and teaching," says Executive Director Sandra Gould.

The children sail on Rhodes 19s, J-22s and Mercury keel boats. They learn basic sail handling and safety on day sailers and then move up. When they become accomplished, they can sail to the outer harbor and into the ocean, as long as they return by sunset. The boats are equipped with VHF radios or (rented) cellular phones in case they need to call for help.

Basic programs are augmented by the U.S. Coast Guard Auxiliary's small boat handling and coastal navigation courses, which the program's students are encouraged to take in the fall and spring.

In 1996, for the first time, the group is targeting adults, who pay $525 for all lessons required to sail a boat safely in the harbor and a membership that lets them "buy" one of twenty boats for six months a year. The boats can be sailed seven days a week, from 10 A.M. to sunset. Members select from several options: two to three hours, a half day or whole day. Membership includes guest speakers and lecturers, barbecues and racing programs.

The organization also helps run the Carroll Center for the Blind's Sail Blind program, a four-prong program where ten to twenty-five blind sailors are paired with sighted helmsmen on Saturdays to sail. Blind students learn to sail at the Center on a working model sailboat by feeling and touching the model. Orientation is in braille and by touch.

Last year, a pilot program for autistic children was launched. These children weren't taught to sail, but received the experience of sailing.

Other children's programs and camps are offered by maritime organizations. In New Orleans, the Maritime and Seafood Industry Museum holds six one-week summer camp sessions for children ages six through thirteen at a cost of $110 a week. The camps combine sailing trips with historic tours, maritime crafts and other activities.

Check with local maritime and nautical museums to see what they offer.

CHILDREN'S SAILING PROGRAMS

Boy Scouts of America
(214) 580-2359
Call local council for sailing information.

Cass' Marina Junior Sailing Program
1702 Bridgeway at Napa St., P.O. Box 643, Sausalito, CA 94966, (415) 332-6789
Eight classes, four days a week on San Francisco Bay. $275 summer eight-day program; $150 spring four-day program.

Community Boating, Inc.
21 Embankment Rd., Boston, MA 02114, (617) 523-1038

Courageous Sailing Center
Boston Harbor, Charlestown Navy Yard, 1 First Ave., Charlestown, MA 02129, (617) 242-3821

Girl Scouts of the U.S.A., Inc.
(800) 223-0624
   Christine Estadrook, Sports Program Consultant

Lake Merritt Adapted Boating Program
Office of Parks and Recreation, 568 Bellevue Ave., Oakland, CA 94610,
(510) 238-2290

Sarasota Youth Sailing Program
742 Hibiscus St., Sarasota, FL 34239, (813) 955-0181

US Sailing
P.O. Box 209, Newport, RI 02840-0209, (401) 849-5200
   Has organized sail racing programs for children, and can provide a list of
community sailing programs for children.

CHAPTER FOUR

CREWING

C rewing offers the best of all worlds at the least possible expense. *Crewing*, being a member of a ship's team, is a way to enjoy sailing and gain sailing experience without the cost of boat ownership; it's a chance to savor the fun without the hassle.

Crew members are usually asked or hired by boat owners to perform certain tasks aboard the boat, tasks that range from cook to navigator to "rail meat," a warm body that acts as ballast (a position that is rarely paid). Crewing may be anything from a short race on the river for an entire racing season to a one-week or several-month journey in an ocean race.

Under the cruising banner, crew members may do an overnight stint, such as a crossing from Florida to the Bahamas, a weekend or two-week cruise to a neighboring town or state, or agree to a year of sailing to faraway ports.

In terms of a career, professional crew members are highly sought, earning from $300 to $600 a week as a mate and from $250 to $400 a week as deckhand on a private yacht. In addition to salary, crew members are fed, housed and provided with an airline ticket home. Of course, salary and benefits vary by size of the boat, boat owner, location of the yacht, duration of the trip and crew member's qualifications.

Another opportunity to crew is on a boat delivery, where a boat owner, agency, broker or manufacturer hires a skipper and crew to take a vessel from one place to another. The trip may be within the U.S. or overseas.

OPTIONS IN RACING

In the racing arena, boat owners who regularly race their boats are always on the lookout for crew. The best opportunities, especially for the novice, are at the local level. For example, Jacksonville, a northeast Florida city spread out along the St. Johns River, boasts a number of yacht clubs and several sailing clubs. The area is home port to an estimated five thousand state-registered sailboats, and fifty or so of those regularly participate in club-sponsored races.

Generally, a boat thirty feet or larger has three crew members plus the skipper. Working through the math, that's roughly 150 crew positions during the racing season. In larger cities, the number of crew members needed is infinitely larger.

Phil and Helen Sullivan are part of the racing regatta. When they traded in their cruising boat for a sleek racer, their immediate quest was for crew members. Though racing was fairly new to them, they asked a number of novice sailors to join them as crew.

"We were looking for compatibility and for people who would commit for the entire season," says Helen. "We were able to put the novices in less-critical areas and help them learn." Though the crew roster was set, when regular crew members couldn't make the race, the Sullivans asked other people to fill the slots.

The Sullivans pay the race entrance fee and provide food, beverages and team T-shirts for their crew. When an overnight stay is required, they also foot the marina bill. On an overnight trip, crew members pay for their own evening meal when dining out, or chip in for a meal on board. The Sullivans are typical of most racing boat owners, according to Helen, who has crewed on other boats. Yet there are a few boat owners who ask the crew to pitch in for beverages or to bring their own.

Joining a sailing club is the best way to find opportunities to crew in your immediate area. Besides yacht clubs, most communities have a number of sailing clubs and organizations. Many clubs accept members who don't own boats, but who have an interest in sailing. Experience is seldom a factor—an interest in the sport is usually sufficient. Through sailing clubs you gain exposure to a variety of sailors, both those who race and those who cruise. Members are often world-class sailors, people who have sailed around the world in races or for pleasure. Experienced sailors love the sport and are happy to share their knowledge with others.

Major sailing centers such as Annapolis, San Francisco and Chicago have crew lists. Racers seeking crew and crew seeking boats to race on post their names and other pertinent information on bulletin boards at yacht clubs and community sailing clubs. There is even a crew list online. Though most requests are for racing, others are seeking cruising adventures.

You can start your search for a sailing club in your area by checking the local yellow pages under Sailing or Organizations. But many clubs operate on a shoestring budget and don't have a telephone listing. Another way to find out about them is to simply "walk the dock" at a marina and ask other sailors. Or check on the bulletin board in the marina office, if it has one. You can also check for the local chapter of the U.S. Power Squadron, whose members will probably know about the area sailing clubs or local marine stores—their salespeople often are sailors.

Being a sailing club member is how one man ended up as a participant in the Southern Ocean Racing Circuit (SORC) race.

Herb belonged to a local sailing club, and his skills as a navigator were well known. A fellow club member decided to enter the SORC. He asked Herb to crew in the position of *navigator*, the person who figures out the boat's position and who plots the course, usually by taking sun, star and moon sights with a sextant. Herb agreed to sail one part of the race, from Miami to Nassau. Herb got off in Nassau and flew home, at his expense, while another crew member got on in Nassau and continued the race.

Herb, who has spent the last twenty years sailing the globe, has also taught sailing and navigation classes. He says opportunities to crew abound. As an example, he cites three students in one of his navigation classes who signed on as paid navigators after completing his course—one of the students went to Africa on a commercial freighter.

In high-profile races, such as the America's Cup, experienced sailors are usually paid to crew. Of course, these are highly sought positions going only to the best sailors who are, in addition, able to take time off from their work and families to participate. But many people work their way up to such positions by becoming knowledgeable and valuable crew members.

Experienced crew members are usually sought out by the boat owner. Extremely competitive owners will go to great lengths to find the best people to fill a specialized position. They often find them by word-of-mouth, asking other professional racers for recommendations. But professional crew members also seek owners out; if they are not well known, the owner may ask for credentials or recommendations.

Racing, especially ocean racing, can be a grueling sport; the beauty of being a crew member is that you usually are responsible for only one job, including taking a turn on *watch* (sailing the boat while other crew members sleep). Crew jobs can range from: "grinder," working the boat's winches; foredeck crew, a sometimes dangerous job that involves handling the head sails and spinnaker; navigator; cook, preparing and serving all the meals; ballast, serving as weight to keep the boat from heeling over too much in stormy or windy weather; or even skipper, the person who sits behind the wheel (or *tiller*) and steers. On a long ocean race, you can sometimes opt for one or two legs of a four- or five-leg voyage.

Competitive, serious boat owners are looking for highly skilled crew, but less-competitive owners may extend an invitation to someone who shows promise but is not a pro. These people are rarely paid for their work, and may even have to help pay for the trip. Whether you are paid or have to help pay is solely dependent upon the boat owner and your decision to accept the offer.

Randy Heath, who sold his sailboat when he moved to Hawaii, learned that crewing is a tradeoff. While he has enjoyed the years of being on the water, both racing and cruising, without the expense, he misses being in command of his own vessel. Yet, he says, "Anywhere I've ever gone in three years, I've never been without a boat. And the cost has been negligible."

CRUISING

If racing isn't to your liking, cruising may well be. The pace is slower and the pleasures can be greater.

As novice boat owners and cruisers, my husband and I decided to take crew along on our first trip to the Bahamas. We chose our crew based on compatibility rather than experience. A male friend owned a powerboat and was studying for a U.S. Coast Guard captain's license, but he knew little about sailing. Another acquaintance, a member of our sailing club, had some experience sailing in the ocean close to shore and on the river, and she was eager for an offshore experience.

Because we planned a twenty-day cruise, both crew members shared the cost of food and beverages, while we paid for fuel and other boat expenses. Our female friend could stay only a week and arranged to fly home from the Bahamas at her expense. Our male friend, who stayed the entire trip, ended up spending about $400 for the three-week vacation.

While a trip to the Bahamas—or almost any country—is within reach of most nonsailors' means and budgets, such trips are often limited to tourist spots. Sailing on a private boat is the only way to see the real Bahamas and its three thousand islands, many of which are paradises inhabited only by coconut palms, sandy white beaches and a few birds and insects. Such islands are surrounded by undersea worlds that few people have seen. That's the lure of cruising, and crewing is the least expensive way to do it.

CRUISING WITH A FAMILY

Many cruisers going on an extended cruise for the first time, or making a long ocean passage, take crew to help them in the event of bad weather, in case someone gets sick, or for companionship. Young couples on an extended voyage with children sometimes seek a nanny or a teacher. Elderly cruisers also may look for crew to help them with heavy tasks. Single men and women often want to share the thrill and beauty of a voyage with like-minded people of either the same or opposite sex. And some cruisers augment their cruising budgets by taking crew who are willing to pay for the experience of a lifetime.

In some instances, cruisers seek someone who can share all of the expenses: fuel, boat repairs and overnight marina fees, as well as food and water. In other cases, they will pay some or all of the costs, including airfare back home. Need is often the determining factor. Some boat owners need someone only to help them with a passage, say from New York to Bermuda. When they get to their destination, they expect the crew member to leave so they can enjoy the destination alone. Crew members can fly back home after reaching the destination, can spend a few weeks or more exploring the area, or can volunteer to crew on yet another boat making a passage elsewhere. They have only to check with other boat owners in the marina or at an anchorage to find a crew position to the next destination. Having money to sustain you in case a boat looking for crew members doesn't materialize immediately is wise.

Sailing experience may not always be a critical factor in selecting crew. An elderly cruiser may seek someone with a great deal of sailing experience, while a couple who needs a cook may only require that you perform the job, are familiar with or comfortable on a boat and are not prone to seasickness. A friend may be willing to teach you the ropes just to have some companionship or to have someone who can help share expenses. And personal ads in sailing magazines abound for men and women who are seeking a companion to make the dream cruise of a lifetime with them.

ARE YOU COMPATIBLE?

In cruising, more so than in racing, compatibility is a key factor. Spending weeks or months on a boat in its limited space can put a strain on family relationships, not to mention the toll it takes on friends and acquaintances; with strangers, it may be even tougher. Both skipper and crew should determine their compatibility long before setting out on a voyage. This can be accomplished by spending a few weekends sailing together on the boat, preferably under sail to a given destination. Yet, even such a limited test may not work. Both crew members and boat owners can attest to "the cruise from hell." One couple spent weeks with a crew member before setting out on a one-month voyage only to find the person had a "Jekyll and Hyde" personality at sea. Crew stories abound about even-tempered friends who turn into Captain Bligh, the commander of the *H.M.S. Bounty* whose crew mutinied, when they go to sea.

Furthermore, if you consider signing on with someone you don't know, or don't know well, you will want to determine the seaworthiness of the boat, whether it has proper safety equipment, and the skill and knowledge of the skipper. This is especially important if you have limited sailing and navigation skills.

The same caveat holds true for those seeking romance or friendship. Investigate your cruising partner thoroughly if you don't know him or her well. What holds true for blind dates on land should hold doubly true for cruising. Be careful. Don't be blind-sided by the magic of cruising to a foreign port and fail to check out the person and the boat you are traveling on.

FINDING CREW POSITIONS

Ways to find crew positions include belonging to sailing clubs, through friends and acquaintances, and through classified or personal ads. Such ads are most readily found in local, state, regional and national sailing publications, many of which are free at boating supply stores and marinas. National consumer magazines such as *SAIL* and *Cruising World*, and the BOAT/U.S. newsletter, which is mailed to members of that national boating organization, frequently contain ads for crew. Occasionally such ads can be found in the classified sections of daily newspapers and in alternative weekly newspapers. Ads are placed by people who want to crew as well as by people looking for crew. (Paying positions for professional crew are discussed later in this chapter.)

FINDING LOVE, ROMANCE AND MARRIAGE

A want ad is how one woman in southwest Florida found a crew member— and a friend. The woman began sailing at age fifty after her husband died. She bought a rather large cruising boat, learned to sail by joining a local sailing club, and found a cruising mate by placing a personal ad in her local newspaper and in regional sailing magazines. She found a man she was compatible with, and they sailed off to Mexico. They returned after three months and, although the cruise didn't lead to romance, they have remained good friends and sailing companions.

For Herb and Mary, a chance meeting at sea led to marriage. Mary was asked by an elderly couple who were members of her California yacht club to help them on a passage from the island of San Andreas to Honduras. When she flew in to the island, she was met at the airport not only by her friends, but by another single sailor who had his own boat whom they had been accompanying from the Panama Canal Zone. By the end of ten days, when her time with the couple was up, Herb, a retired doctor, had asked her to accompany him on his cruise.

Theirs was "an instant attraction," according to Herb. Four dozen Central American countries and two-and-a-half years later they were married.

THE BENEFITS

Crewing has other advantages as well. It's an inexpensive way to find out if you really enjoy the sport. There's nothing sadder than a new sailor with a boat that never leaves the marina because the owner found out he didn't like sailing after all. If you find yourself frequently seasick on ocean cruises or races, but enjoy sailing nonetheless, you will have learned to limit your sailing to rivers, lakes and other sheltered bodies of water (or to find a remedy for seasickness, of which there are many). When you're ready to buy a boat of your own, you'll know from such a deduction exactly what to look for. Instead of a large, ocean-going sailboat, you can purchase a smaller one more suitable for inland waterways and coastal passages.

Another plus to crewing first and buying later is the opportunity to sail on boats of different types and sizes from a variety of manufacturers. You can "test-drive" different boats under varying conditions before you buy. But most of all, crewing is a chance to gain the experience needed to skipper your own boat.

Rick started his sailing adventures that way. After learning to sail, he bought a small boat and sailed mostly on a sheltered river. Before purchasing a larger boat and taking to the ocean, he crewed on a variety of boats both inshore and offshore. What he gained was the experience and confidence to sail offshore by himself, and the opportunity to discount boats he didn't like. Finally he purchased a larger boat, fully intending to one day sail the boat to the Virgin Islands. He realized his dream two years later when, assisted by a crew member, he took to the sea. He has been happily living and working in the Caribbean for more than three years.

CREW MEMBER RESPONSIBILITIES

"The captain, in the first place, is lord paramount. He stands no watch, comes and goes when he pleases, is accountable to no one, and must be obeyed in everything, without a question even from his chief officer."

Richard Henry Dana, Two Years Before the Mast

When it comes to safety, skippers are responsible for their boat *and* the crew, but crew members have responsibilities, too. As cruisers, they are expected to bring their own safety gear, including a life vest, lifeline and clothing suitable for cold or wet weather; if they have special needs for food, drink or medications, they are expected to take care of those as well. They should become familiar with the boat and how it operates, and learn about their intended destinations and the route. They should learn to operate all safety equipment on the boat, including radios and navigation devices. Even though the job may not be assigned to them, if one person on the boat gets sick, has a heart attack, breaks a leg or arm, or any other emergency arises, they may have to fill in on a moment's notice. Usually, there are fewer crew members on a cruising boat than on one that is racing. That means more work for each of the crew, and more varied duties. Of course, exceptions abound.

Race crew should show up for each race on time, or notify the skipper if something arises that prevents them from participating. Nothing aggravates a captain more than sitting at the dock before the start of a race waiting on a late crew member. Many boat owners will leave the tardy member behind.

A positive attitude, a willingness to learn, and pitching in from time to time to help with boat chores go a long way toward earning a berth aboard any boat.

In short, the most valued crew members are not necessarily those who know it all, or who even specialize in a certain area, such as sail handling. Rather, they're the people who are constantly learning to improve their skills, who get along well with others in close quarters, and who show a willingness to help and join in on the fun—and the work.

PROFESSIONAL CREW

People who crew for a living often register with an agency to find a position that may last for a few weeks or a year or more.

These agencies, which operate like temporary employment agencies, specialize in boating crew and often advertise in sailing magazines. They are either seeking boat owners to use their services or crew members to fill positions. They also hire very capable, proven sailors to deliver boats for owners from one destination to the next. Often the person hired to make a delivery is paid a lump sum that includes money to hire additional crew as helpers. While you may not be the one to get the job, you may be hired by someone else to help—and get paid for doing so.

A sampling of positions, pay, duties and experience, provided by Ami Griffith of Crew Unlimited in Fort Lauderdale, Florida, and Newport, Rhode Island, follows. Crew Unlimited specializes in finding full-time crew for positions on board powerboats and sailboats that range in size from 90 to 130 feet.

CREW TITLES AND PAY RANGES

Captain Manages all crew members and is responsible for the boat. Moves the boat from one place to another, acts as liaison for boat owner between crew, shipyard and marinas. Weekly pay range: $500 to $2,000.

Chef Responsible for planning meals, cooking and stocking food. Weekly pay range: $500 to $800.

Chief Steward Manages stewards. Keeps vessel stocked with supplies ranging from toiletries to liquor. Weekly pay range: $350 to $800.

Deckhand Keeps boat exterior clean, handles lines. Weekly pay range: $250 to $400.

Engineer In charge of boat systems, such as engine, generator and air-conditioning. Weekly pay range: $500 to $1,000.

Mate In charge of maintaining exterior, and sometimes supervising deck-hands. Helps with navigation and reports to captain. Weekly pay range: $300 to $600.

Steward/Stewardess Cares for the boat's interior. Cleans, serves meals to owners and guests, does laundry. Weekly pay range: $300 to $450.

OPPORTUNITIES FOR NOVICES

While many paid positions go to seasoned, experienced professionals, there are opportunities for novices, who may then work their way up to better positions. To be considered by a crew agency, you will need to submit a resume that details boating experience, work experience, references and copies of any certification you may have. People without formal yachting experience who have mechanical aptitude or experience in the service industry have the best chances of getting accepted by a crew agency, despite their lack of sailing ability.

Crewing as a career can be fun and rewarding; it's also a hard life that takes you away from family, friends and home for extended periods. This often includes time away during holidays such as Christmas. Chefs and stewards stay in their positions six months to one year on average.

Moreover, benefits may stop at salary. An estimated 85 percent of all private yachts are not registered in the U.S., so the owners do not have to pay worker's compensation insurance, federal and state withholding taxes or unemployment taxes. For crew, this usually means no health insurance, no retirement and little or no Social Security to fall back on.

These shortcomings have been recognized within the industry and are being addressed.

Crew agencies advertise in sailing magazines and newspapers, and there are listings in the yellow pages under Boating, Yacht Crew and similar headings. Most agencies are based in large sailing centers: Fort Lauderdale, Florida; Newport, Rhode Island; Annapolis, Maryland; Antibes, France; San Francisco, California; Seattle, Washington; and throughout the Caribbean, especially in the Virgin Islands. You may also learn about opportunities from other professionals, yacht owners, boatyards and marinas, and manufacturers and builders.

BOAT DELIVERIES

Many accomplished sailors, usually those who have a captain's license, make a living and see the world transporting other people's boats from one place to another. The delivery may involve helping a boat owner with little blue-water experience take the boat to a specific location such as Europe, Puerto Rico or Hawaii. The boat owner pays a lump sum or a daily rate, and provides food, lodging and airfare home when the trip is over.

Sometimes a boat owner may not have the time to take his boat from New York to the Caribbean during the winter, and will pay someone to deliver the boat to a specific marina. Or a boat broker may hire someone to deliver a boat to a customer or to a boat show.

In all these instances, the delivery person is usually required to have a captain's license, because that person will be completely in charge of the vessel. Even with a captain's license, the boat owner may be looking for experience and familiarity in sailing to the destination. A captain whose sole experience is coastal sailing would probably not be a good candidate for delivery from the U.S. to Europe. And one who has sailed from Florida to the Caribbean a dozen times may not be a good candidate to sail a boat from New York to Nova Scotia, or from California to British Columbia. The decision rests with the person doing the hiring.

Boat captains are licensed by *tonnage*, the weight of the vessel. As a rule, the larger the boat, the more it weighs. Once a captain is hired, he may want to in turn hire crew to help him, especially if the boat is large or the destination is far away. The boat owner may provide enough money for crew and leave the decision of who to hire to the captain, or the owner may hire his own crew and ask the captain to work with them.

A boat delivery is usually not a pleasure trip, though it can be pleasurable. For the most part, the boat has to be at a specific point on a specific date, and delivery captains and crew generally run nonstop to the destination. So in many cases, the crew hired has to be knowledgeable and competent. But if the crew is large and experienced, a novice with aptitude may be considered.

Finding a position as crew on a yacht delivery is basically the same procedure as finding any other position: word of mouth, sailing schools, reputation, classified advertisements and so on.

Tania Aebi and Olivier Berner, who own Varakka Deliveries, supplement their income by delivering other people's yachts. The couple rose to fame when Tania, at age sixteen, set out on a 26-foot sailboat with little advanced sailing experience to circumnavigate the globe alone. She chronicled her trip for *Cruising World* magazine. During the trip, she met Olivier, a single-handed sailor on an ocean voyage. When she returned to New York, she wrote a book about her adventure, *Maiden Voyage*, and she and Olivier married. They now live in Vermont and have two children.

Despite the vast experience she gained sailing around the world, Tania got a captain's license when she returned. She and Olivier deliver a few boats a year, mostly for private yacht owners.

"I'm sure people can make a living delivering boats, but you have to be closer to the boating world and work with a broker. We have to do other things to supplement our earnings, but deliveries are part of what we do," she says.

According to Tania, some of the drawbacks are not knowing the boat you will sail on and having to hurry to reach a destination.

"You don't get rich off of it," she says, "and it's a side job for most people."

CREWING
Captains and Crew
Virgin Islands, (809) 776-2395

Coral Bay Connections
P.O. Box 9901, St. John, U.S. Virgin Islands 00830-9726, (809) 779-4994

Crew Finders
404 SE Seventeenth St., Fort Lauderdale, FL 33316, (800) GET-CREW

Crew Unlimited
Ft. Lauderdale, FL, (305) 462-4624; Newport, RI, (401) 847-8110

Cruz Bay
P.O. Box 37, St. John, U.S. Virgin Islands 00831, (809) 776-6922

The Detroit Area Crew List
E-mail: jrmuniz@hooked.net

Hassel Free Crew Placement
404 SE Seventeenth St., Ft. Lauderdale, FL 33316, (305) 763-1841

New York Area Racing Crew List
website: http://www.walrus.com/~belov/crewlist.html

San Francisco Bay Area Racing Crew List
website: http://www.hooked.net/users/jrmuniz/crew//st.html

Online site that takes requests to crew in races on San Francisco Bay. Give name, date or dates available, telephone number and preferred positions. Novices can check "any area is okay." Experience level: beginner to professional.

The Seattle Crew List
E-mail: junkins@u.washington.edu
website: http://weber.u.Washington.edu/junkins

Listings of skippers looking for crew, including name and telephone number, e-mail address, location of boat, type and name of boat and rating, positions looking for and experience level seeking. Also individual notes from skippers and requests for crew for cruises and long-distance offshore races.

CHAPTER FIVE

CHARTERING AND RENTING

"The only record I would cherish would be for the longest circumnavigation, the most dilly-dallying on the way."
Gwenda Cornell, Pacific Odyssey

Chartering is a way to sail the world without the cost of buying, equipping and outfitting a sailboat and taking off a year or more to do it.

Those who dream of sailing into a reef-fringed lagoon in Tahiti, cruising the canals of France or tying up to a harbor wall in Greece can fulfill the dream on someone else's boat.

Even sailboat owners find chartering the lure of a sweet siren song. They can spend weekends in their hometown on their own boat, and summer vacations in far-flung foreign ports.

But chartering isn't just for far-away vacations. Those who enjoy sailing but don't want the responsibilities of boat ownership or don't have enough time to sail to make owning a boat a smart venture find chartering meets their needs. From Martha's Vineyard to the San Juan Islands to the sunny Florida Keys and coast of Maine, charter companies offer cruising vacations stateside as well.

Chartering and renting are the same thing—paying to take a boat owned by someone else out sailing. Both are often done by the same companies, but, in general, renting is usually a short-term endeavor, by the hour, half-day or day, while chartering involves trips of two days or more.

Renting is a good way to see a new part of the country when you have reached the destination by car or air. It's also a good way to "test" sailboat models, to continue sailing when you're in between boats and, for novices, a way to see if you even *like* sailing.

Charter companies usually offer two basic services: *bareboat*, where you take the boat out by yourself, just as if it were your own, or *crewed*, where you hire people to sail the boat for you. Some of the largest charter companies also offer a third option, a *berth*, which is like sailing on a cruise ship on a much smaller scale. You pay for a spot on the boat and share the boat with other people whom you may not know, while captain and crew do all the work. Another option at some companies is a bareboat with just a skipper aboard to help you out if you get in trouble or until you feel confident about sailing the charter boat or in an area new to you and unlike the area in which you've sailed. For example, if you've sailed for years on a lake, you may not be comfortable sailing in the ocean, even though you know how to sail.

Though chartering may be a cost effective alternative to boat ownership, it certainly isn't cheap. A typical charter can range from $700 to $2,000 a week in season in the U.S., and from $1,000 to $4,000 a week throughout the world. What determines the price? Location, company, type and size of boat, number of people and number of days chartered.

The secrets to budget chartering are off-season trips, chartering with a handpicked group of friends to share the cost of the boat and using "Mom and Pop" charter companies.

To charter a boat on your own (*bareboating*), you must prove to the charter company that you are qualified to sail a boat approximately the size of the one you intend to charter in conditions similar to where you will charter from. Proof may include previous boat ownership, certification from approved sailing courses or a written or onboard test given by the company dockside.

Some charter companies may restrict how far you may take their boat, and of course the length of time chartered for will determine how far you can go. Some companies offer a "drop off" service, where you drop the boat off at a destination other than where you picked it up. This allows you more time to cover new ground than if you have to return the boat to the place where you boarded. It also usually costs more.

American-flagged charter boats must have certain safety equipment required by the U.S. Coast Guard on board, but many charter boats are not registered in the U.S. Find out ahead of time what safety gear is on the boat and what you may have to bring. Some charter companies often provide "toys" such as wind surfers, snorkel gear or personal watercraft. Again, ask before you sign—there may be a charge for these goodies.

PROVISIONING

Unlike a cruise ship, bareboat charters do not include food. You may get a good rate on the boat, only to learn that you must provision (stock food) from the charter company, and the cost can be high, especially in foreign ports. But most charter companies give you the option of doing your own provisioning.

If you decide to bring food from the States, you must weigh the cost of bringing it in and the possibility of paying duty on it, not to mention the hassle of carting canned goods from home to airplane to taxi to boat.

Letting the charter company provision for you also saves you the time of hiring transportation to a grocery store (if there is one) in foreign ports, not to mention facing sticker shock. In the Bahamas and many other island nations, everything is flown in, which increases the cost of all purchased items 30 percent or more. Sometimes it pays to let the company provision for you, even if the costs seem high. And a few charter companies will give you a choice of menus, from basic to gourmet.

COMPATIBILITY

If you do decide to gather a group of friends to share the cost of a bareboat charter with you, make sure you're compatible in a small space for a week. Many a friendship has been ruined at sea because of the close living quarters. After all, you're sharing living space on a boat forty-four feet long by twelve feet wide, on average. That's not much room for four to six people. Spend time on a boat with your friends *before* you go chartering, determining who will do what. Each person can rotate between captain, cook and deckhand.

CREWED CHARTERS

If you're new to sailing in general, as well as chartering, you may be more comfortable on a crewed yacht, suggests Michael Ann Harvey, public relations director for Clearwater, Florida-based The Moorings, one of the largest chartering companies in the world. The company has twenty-three bases: in the U.S., the Caribbean, the South Pacific, the Mediterranean and the Sea of Cortez, in the Baha area of Mexico.

A crewed yacht gives you "a taste of the sailing lifestyle at $995 a person, which includes meals and bar beverages, in the off season. Although the captain will not teach you to sail, he may allow you a turn at the wheel and allow you to help sail the ship, if you want to. From him, you will pick up cruising tips and learn about local-knowledge anchorages, nightspots and restaurants, and pristine islands and snorkeling areas.

Chartering in the off-season can save you as much as 45 percent. In the Caribbean, the off-season is June through September, primarily because of hurricane season. But the bonus is that the weather is slightly cooler and crowded anchorages are uncommon. While hurricanes are a real and dangerous threat, most years they are few and far between.

Another chartering option is to rent a bareboat and hire a captain at a daily rate, about $90 a day. The Moorings has a "friendly skipper" program for people who have never chartered with them before. You receive a free day of chartering if you hire a skipper for that one day. The skipper sits by and offers advice while you gain confidence with the boat, or helps you get started.

"You are responsible for feeding him and bringing him back, but he's yours for the day," Harvey says. Or you can keep him on at the daily rate, if you desire.

Whether you enjoy your first-time charter will also depend on your skills and where you go. In the Bahamas, the British Virgin Islands and Tonga, sailing is in a protected area and you are always within sight of land. For the most part, the waters are calm and protected. There are more shops, grocery stores and nightlife, with the bonus of nearby deserted islands with palm trees and sandy beaches. But in other areas, like St. Lucia or the Grenadines, you're more exposed to ocean swells, which make some people uncomfortable.

PRIVATE BOAT CHARTERS

Another way to charter inexpensively is to go with a private-boat owner. Popular cruising destinations, such as California, Florida, the Bahamas and the Caribbean, are filled with people who are willing to provide a crewed charter to earn extra money. Some do it occasionally, and some buy their boat with chartering in mind.

Such is the case of Roger and Alicia Page, who quit their jobs, sold their belongings and bought a boat to charter in St. Marten. They charter the boat part of the year, in the "high" season, and leisurely cruise the remainder of the year.

For someone who wants to charter from a private-boat owner, the savings are 30 to 40 percent off what charter companies charge. The experience, however, may be a mixed blessing. Overall, most private-boat owners take great pride in their boats because it's their home, so the boat you get will probably be in *Bristol* (perfect) condition; a handful may be desperate for money to make needed repairs, and the boat may not be as seaworthy or as cosmetically nice as it could be. But then, that's the chance you take even with a larger charter company. Some companies are not well managed, and the boats break down or may not be in prime condition.

Before you charter, ask for information about the boat and for a picture. But be aware that the picture may have been taken five or even ten years earlier. When you reach the boat, check it over carefully and ensure that everything is in working condition. Word of mouth is the best way to learn about good, small companies or private-boat owners.

The other plus to chartering with a private-boat owner is personal service. The drawback is that response to your inquiry may not be as quick as you may like.

TIP:

Ask about a "first time" discount. Some charter companies offer a special package rate on a one-week charter, which includes airfare and one-night hotel accommodations, for people who are chartering for the first time.

Finding a company or private boat to charter is very simple: Open any consumer sailing magazine. Charter companies advertise heavily, and most magazines have an index to advertisers under specific headings. Also, most sailing magazines have at least an annual section on chartering. You'll find private charters in the classified section under a variety of headings: Wanted, Positions, Charters and Rentals. Also check with your friends, or on the Internet's World Wide Web pages under charters or individual countries or islands. You might also check with hotels in the area you want to charter in, or the booths of people who sell day trips and other activities. In the States, look on marina bulletin boards and in local sailing publications.

Few private charterers outside of the States have toll-free reservation numbers—in fact, few have telephones—because of the expense and poor communications systems. But they often have a facsimile number, and that's the cheapest, fastest and easiest way to reach them.

Another alternative to chartering is through a private individual who doesn't really charter, but who occasionally offers one- or two-week cruises to nearby destinations.

Such is the case with Jim of Cape Coral, Florida, who has been taking paying passengers from his home port to the Dry Tortugas for twelve years on his Soverel 37.

Jim, who advertises in sailing magazines, says he has logged over fifty thousand miles since 1980. He charges $600 a week per person for the seven-day Dry Tortugas trip, which includes stops in Key West and the Marquesas Islands.

"I'm not really big enough to make a living at it," he says, "but it helps pay for the maintenance of the boat."

Most passengers know how to sail, or own a small sailboat that they sail on a lake. They come as paying crew to learn more about ocean sailing or celestial navigation (navigating by the sun, moon and stars). A few, he says, are just along for the ride.

You'll find similar ads for paying crew and guests to sail around the world,

TIP:

Some charter companies provide a discount for booking a charter at the last minute, if they have boats available in the fleet. Ask.

to the Caribbean, to Mexico and to Hawaii. Typically, boats departing the east coast are headed for Bermuda, Nova Scotia and Europe; those heading for the Caribbean will advertise in Florida. For Mexico, boats depart regularly from the west coast of Florida, California or the Gulf states. Boats from California are usually headed for Hawaii and the South Pacific; from Washington, to the San Juan Islands and British Columbia or south to California and the Baha coast.

Even magazines offer charters. *Cruising World*, for example, offers limited charters to a limited number of people to worldwide destinations at excellent rates. An October 1996 cruise to Fiji included round-trip airfare from Los Angeles, hotel accommodations, ten days of sailing, full provisions, lead boat with a skipper, guides, transfers, fuel and water—all for about $3,350 per person.

CHARTER BROKERS

If you don't feel confident making the chartering decision yourself, you might consider a charter broker or agent. Charter brokers work like travel agents— they help the buyer make decisions about destinations and accommodations.

"Some charter operations are really shabby; some are really good," says Ed Hamilton, owner of the company that bears his name. "There isn't one company that's good for everyone."

Hamilton's company, in business for twenty-three years, gathers information from the client: destination, boat type and size desired, length of time, date, experience and other factors. Based on that information, he sends them a list of all the charter companies, small and large, in the area they are considering, as well as color brochures. After the prospective charterers have had time to study the material, Hamilton or one of his agents reviews it with them and the decision is made. There is no fee for the service; the agency receives commissions from charter companies, airlines and hotels.

Hamilton's services go even further than that. The package of information he sends includes tips and advice on provisioning and lists of supermarkets.

Such an agency may save a charterer money, but the service is a convenience. "It's a grave mistake to make such a decision just on price," he warns. "Our job is to explain what they will get for their money so they won't be surprised when they get there."

CHARTER BROKERS

Ed Hamilton & Company
P.O. Box 430, Whitefield, ME 04353, (800) 621-7855

Jubilee Yacht Charters
(800) 922-4871

Sailing Vacations, Inc.
(800) 922-4880

CHARTER COMPANIES

(This is not an inclusive list, but a sampling. Note that some foreign charter companies have stateside offices, and some charter companies may be based in one state but offer charters in a variety of states and/or countries.)

Adventure Sail Hawaii
P.O. Box 44335, Kamuela, HI 96743, (800) 726-7245

Anacortes Yacht Charter
Anacortes, WA, (800) 233-3004

Bay Breeze Yacht Charters
12935 W. Bayshore Dr., Suite 200, Traverse City, MI 49684, (616) 941-0535

Bellhaven Charters
#9 Squalicum Mall, Bellingham, WA 98225, (800) 542-8812

Blue Pacific Yacht Charters
1519 Foreshore Walk, Vancouver, BC V6H 3X3, Canada, (800) 237-2392

Bosun's Charters, Ltd.
P.O. Box 2464C, Sidney, BC V8L 3Y3, Canada, (604) 656-6644

Canadian Yacht Charters
Gore Bay, ON, Canada, (800) 565-0022

Caribbean Sailing Charters, Inc.
3883 Andrews Crossing, Roswell, GA 30075, (800) 824-1331

Caribbean Yacht Charters
Marblehead, MA, (800) 225-2520

Charter Cats of the Bahamas
Fleet H.Q, Hatchet Bay, Eleuthera, Bahamas, (809) 335-0186

Charters Northwest
1171 Fairview Ave., N., Seattle, WA 98109, (206) 682-5484

Chelsea Yacht Charters
P.O. Box 10, Chelsea, NY 12512, (800) 892-1605

Cooper Boating Center
1620 Duranleau St., Granville Island, Vancouver, BC V6H 3S4, Canada

Corpus Christi SS
Corpus Christi, TX, (512) 881-8583

Desolation Sound Yacht Charters, Ltd.
#201-1797 Comox Ave., Comox, BC V9M 3L9, Canada, (604) 339-7222

Freedom Charters
305 Oliphant Lane, Middletown, RI 02842, (800) 999-2909

Good Time Charters NV
Alicia and Roger Page, c/o The Mailbox, P.O. Box 523882, Miami, FL
33152-3882, Morgan 46, *Flying Eagle*

GPSC Charters
Philadelphia, PA, (215) 247-3903

Hawaii Sailing Co.
P.O. Box 1813, Honokaa, HI 96727, (808) 326-1986

Hinckley Yacht Charters
P.O. Box 10, Bass Harbor Marine, Bass Harbor, ME 04653, (800) 492-7245

Honolulu Sailing Co.
47-335 Lulani St., Kaneohe, HI 96744, (800) 829-0114

Interpac Yachts, Inc.
1050 Anchorage Lane, San Diego, CA 92106, (619) 222-0327

King Yacht Charters
Tonga, Fiji, New Zealand, Tahiti, New Caledonia, Australia,
(800) 521-7552

Marina Sailing
California, (800) 262-7245

The Moorings
19345 U.S. Hwy. 19 N., 4th Floor, Clearwater, FL 34624, (800) 535-7289

North Huron Charters
1266 Queen St., E., Sault Ste. Marie, ON T6A 2E8, Canada

North Sailing Charters
P.O. Box 32391, Juneau, AK 99803

North South Yacht Charters
655 Dixon Rd., Suite 18, Toronto, ON M9W 1J4, Canada, (800) 387-4964

Offshore Sailing
16731-110 McGregor Blvd., Fort Myers, FL 33908, (800) 221-4326

Passage Charter Co.
306 Main St., Suite 317, Ketchikan, AK 99901, (907) 225-8551

Penmar Marine Company Yacht Charters
2011 Skyline Way, Anacortes, WA 98221

Sailboats, Inc.
250 Marina Dr., Superior, WI 54880, (800) 826-7010

Sailing Center of Santa Barbara
(800) 350-9090

San Diego Yacht Charters
(800) 456-0222

San Juan Sailing
Bellingham, WA, (800) 677-7245

Seabreeze Yacht Charters
Toronto, ON, Canada, (800) 668-2807

Stardust Marine
2280 University Dr., Suite 102, Newport Beach, CA 92660, (800) 634-8822

Sunsail Charters
115 E. Broward Blvd., Fort Lauderdale, FL 33301, (800) 327-2276

Sun Yacht Charters
59 B Union St., P.O. Box 737, Camden, ME 04843, (800) 772-3503

Superior Charters
Rt. 1, P.O. Box 719, Bayfield, WI 54814, (800) 772-5124

Tradewind Yacht Charters
Glouster, VA, (800) 825-7245

Tropic Island Yacht Charters
Maya Cove, Tortola, (800) 356-8938

U-Sail-It, Inc.
P.O. Box 54, Colchester, VT 05446, (802) 878-8888

Waltzing Bear Sail Charters
4600 Halibut Point Rd., Sitka, AK 99835

Whitsunday Sailing Charters
P.O. Box 599, Whitsunday, Queensland 4802, Australia, (617) 946-1116

RENTING

It is possible to rent a sailboat for a few hours, a half day or a full day, but considering the speed, a half day tends to be the norm for all but the smallest, fastest boats, such as a Hobie catamaran. A rental may be on a small sailboat, ten to sixteen feet, or on a large sailboat of thirty feet or more.

Unlike the charter category, where you take a large, expensive boat out overnight or longer, rental companies may not be as picky about your sailing experience. In a small, sheltered bay, the rental company may even give you free shoreside lessons and let you go. Others may require proof of sailing instruction.

Small sailboat rentals are most commonly found in sheltered waterways, such as inland lakes, small rivers and the bays of areas that draw a heavy tourist trade. The boats are usually Sunfish or Sailfish, good beginner boats, or Hobies, small catamarans that "fly" through the water. Renting a small sailboat is another good way to test your skills and see how much you like sailing.

You'll find rentals listed in the yellow pages under Boats, Boating, Sailboat Rentals or Charters. Other places to find rentals include naval bases on the water (usually restricted to active-duty and retired military members and their families) and community boating clubs (listed in chapter 2).

In Coconut Grove, Florida, Easy Sailing finds its customers tend to be locals with family visiting who want to show them the town by water, or people who rent for a special occasion such as a birthday or an anniversary.

In the San Francisco Bay area, Cass' Marina rents sailboats by the hour, half day or day. Sample rates are $40 an hour to $125 a day for a Santana 22 on weekends, and about 15 percent less for the same boat on weekdays. Rentals are a good way for sailors visiting other areas to see the sights by water.

Similarly, tourist areas are a great place to go to find a crewed rental for about $25 a person. Destinations such as Seattle, Washington, and St. Augustine, Florida, have day and sunset cruises. Sail Seattle departs from Pier 56 at the Seattle Central Waterfront for one-and-a-half hour cruises on a 70-foot sailboat; the price is $20 a person. A two-and-a-half hour sunset cruise is $35 per person.

BOAT RENTALS
Cass' Marina
1702 Bridgeway at Napa St., P.O. Box 643, Sausalito, CA 94966, (415) 332-6789
Rents day-sailers and cruising boats for sails on the delta.

Club Nautique
1150 Ballena Blvd., Alameda, CA 94501, (800) 343-SAIL
Sailing school and rental/charter fleet with four membership levels. Members pay an initiation fee and a monthly fee.

Easy Sailing
P.O. Box 95, Coconut Grove, FL 33133, (800) 783-4001
Day-sailers on Biscayne Bay. Sample rates: 19-foot, $18 an hour, $105 a day; 28-foot, $25 an hour, $140 a day.

The Moorings Sailing Club
St. Petersburg, FL
Members pay $350 initiation fee and $35 a month. Sign up for scheduled events and pay nominal cost, about $5. 25 percent discount on boat rentals.

Naval Air Station Jacksonville
Morale Welfare and Recreation Dept., Bldg. 621, P.O. Box 1, Jacksonville, FL 32212, (904) 772-3260

Pacific Yachting and Sailing
790 Mariner Park Way, Santa Cruz, CA 95062, (800) 374-2626
Member and nonmember rentals. Sample rate: O'Day 27, $160 a day, weekends.

Sail Seattle
P.O. Box 31874, Seattle, WA 98103, (206) 624-3931

CHAPTER SIX

JOINT OWNERSHIP

I f you can't afford the boat you want or you don't want full responsibility for boat ownership, consider owning a boat with someone else. That someone could be a friend, family member, acquaintance or stranger—it might even be a corporation with a special program, often called *charter management*. Though the latter is not a true joint ownership, where both owners share the cost of the boat and expenses equally, such programs can enable you to buy a bigger or better boat than you might otherwise be able to afford on your own. And for a limited time, usually four years or more, charter commissions may help make your boat payment.

Friendship: "A ship big enough to carry two in fair weather, but only one in foul."
Ambrose Bierce, The Devil's Dictionary

Joint ownership with an individual means sharing not only the cost of buying the boat, but also the cost of insurance, upkeep and maintenance, costs easily divided. Determining who will get the boat on which days, weekends and holidays is when problems can arise. But with a well-thought-out plan and good partners, joint ownership can work. The key is preplanning.

The most important part is determining who will be the joint owners. If the co-owners are in the same area and number only two or three, you will probably see each other fairly often and will want people who are compatible. A fastidious sailor coupled with a laid-back one may not work. The former may be intent on keeping the boat in Bristol condition (not a bad idea), and the latter may want to let the little things go and to focus more on enjoying sailing. The owners should be financially stable, responsible and, of course, willing. Things to consider when looking for a partner to buy a boat together:

• Are you both cruisers? Is one of you a racer at heart? A racer will want a competitive boat with racing gear, the cruiser will lean more toward comfort and amenities.

- Can you both afford the monthly payment (if you finance the boat), the insurance, dockage and maintenance?

How can you find a partner? There are a number of ways.

- Advertise in or read classified ads in sailing magazines and newspapers.
- Ask family members, co-workers, friends and acquaintances if they are interested in co-owning a sailboat with you.
- Check marina and sailing club bulletin boards and newsletters.

Once you've found an appropriate partner, together you will have to decide what type and size boat will serve both of your needs, assuming neither of you already owns a boat. This is an important decision, too, because you will each have your own ideas about the ideal boat, and your dreams may differ. If your heart is set on a 40-foot boat that sleeps six for a long-distance cruise each summer, and your partner has always wanted a lower maintenance 26-footer for weekend trips, you may have problems. Compromise is the key here.

Sometimes you may not have to go looking for a partner. You may find a person looking for someone to take on partial ownership of an existing boat. Such offers usually are found in classified advertisements in local, regional or national sailing magazines. This may make some of the above decisions easier. For one, the boat is already determined. You only have to decide if it's a boat you would want to own half of. The rest of the decisions must still be made, the same as if you started from scratch.

Samples of ads for joint ownership:

Three partners looking for fourth in co-ownership of 45' Gulfstar sloop berthed in Tortola, BVI.

Wanted: Partner(s) looking to purchase 28- to 30-ft. sloop to keep in Annapolis, South River area. Mostly for cruising, some interest in racing.

25 percent share available of a 41' Dickerson center cockpit ketch kept year round at Tortola, BVI. Join a four-person partnership in a classic, fully equipped blue-water boat. 25K investment plus one quarter of ongoing expenses.

Here are a few other ways to find a potential partner:

- Check bulletin boards at marinas for boats for sale. If you find one you like, ask the owner if she is interested in joint ownership instead of selling. A boat owner may sell a boat because she no longer has the time to spend on maintenance and sailing or can no longer afford the boat, and may welcome a joint owner rather than selling after all.

- Talk to marina managers; a boat owner may tell him his problems, and finances or lack of time may be some of them. The marina manager may be willing to give you the names and telephone numbers of people who might be willing to share their boat.

People who have been a joint owner have had good and bad experiences; here are two examples of joint ownership that have worked.

A California woman had a happy experience owning her first boat with her sister and brother-in-law after buying a two-year-old Cascade 29 in 1966 for $4,000 cash each. They split expenses for all maintenance and upkeep costs. They had no formal contract, but set a schedule giving each use of the boat every other weekend, regardless of holidays, and two summer weeks for vacations. Boat rules: Whoever last used the boat was responsible for cleaning it.

They shared life jackets and foul-weather gear, and jointly purchased dishes, pots and pans and cooking utensils that stayed on the boat. They set up a kitty for staples such as coffee, sugar and flour, which also were left on board. Occasionally they even exchanged babysitting so the parents could have an "adults only" weekend.

Four years later, the woman sold the boat to her sister and brother-in-law for what she had paid, plus half the cost of improvements.

A more formal approach works well among strangers. William Eiman of Philadelphia, Pennsylvania, has led a ten-person ownership group for about ten years. The group formed a corporation to "own" a boat that it keeps in Red Hook, St. Thomas. Each person owns ten shares of the corporation, which represent one-tenth of the boat's purchase price. Annual assessments shared equally by all members go for operating costs. Members attend several meetings a year to make decisions about the boat's maintenance and the boating schedule. Each owner gets four weeks on the boat, two weeks in the winter and two weeks in the summer.

When a member decides to sell his shares, the owners advertise in sailing magazines for a new owner. Over the years, owners have lived in Louisiana, New York, Illinois, Maryland and Washington, DC. Compatibility is rarely a problem, according to Eiman, because they don't sail together.

"It has worked very, very well," he says. "The annual assessment is less than it would cost to charter the boat for one week. I would recommend it to anyone. I firmly believe that a boat can be used by more than one person. It makes sense to share the costs and the time. This has been an enormously successful thing."

The corporation's last boat was damaged in a 1995 hurricane, and the owners are now buying a used boat to replace it, at a cost of about $13,000 each for a $130,000 boat.

LOOK BEFORE YOU LEAP

Before you sign on the dotted line together, draw up or have your attorneys draw up a partnership agreement. The agreement should spell out every possible contingency and should address these issues:

- How much, or what share, each partner will pay for slip rental, boat insurance, state and federal fees and licenses for the owners and the boat, boat payments or cash purchase.
- Who will pay for accidental or negligent damage to the boat.
- Whether one partner should be reimbursed for providing qualified labor, and the rate to be paid.
- How time on the boat, including vacations and holidays, will be divided among owners.
- Whether boat chores and maintenance will be hired out or performed by owners. If the latter, a schedule of who does what and when.
- What allowances will be made for owners whose vacation periods are set by their companies.
- How requests for extended cruising will be handled.
- Whether an owner is allowed to race the boat.
- The amount, extent and breadth of hull and liability insurance coverage, including deductibles.
- Restrictions on range (one hundred miles offshore or inland waters only) for qualified sailors.
- Guest liability.
- Where the boat will be kept and how it will be stored.
- Job transfers within a certain radius of where the boat is kept, if applicable.
- Sale of ownership shares: whether the partners should have to approve a buyer, and inability to sell contingencies.
- Share buyouts. How the sale will be arranged and the basis for price.

All of these questions will have to be resolved, preferably in writing, before you buy the boat. Be sure you arrive at answers for all possible contingencies before you enter a partnership.

CHARTER MANAGEMENT

Another form of joint ownership is placing your boat into a charter management program. A number of charter companies have plans that allow you to purchase a boat, put it into charter service for a specified period, share a percentage of the income earned from charters and return the boat to you after a specified period, usually no longer than five years.

During the contract period, you are allowed a certain number of weeks per year on your boat, on another boat in the fleet at the charter point or at another charter point. For example, you place the boat for charter in the Virgin Islands, but you can take your allotted time on another boat in another place, say the Bahamas.

Charter companies that offer such plans advertise in sailing magazines and attend boat shows.

Such programs also are offered by yacht management companies. Unlike charter programs, which sometimes require that you buy a boat from them or their manufacturer, or to their specifications, management programs allow you to select your own boat and they manage charters for you.

Be aware that all of these programs require formal legal contracts. A new boat large enough to charter costs $125,000 and up; this is a major investment and a major financial liability. This form of partnership also may have income tax implications. The contract should not be entered into lightly. It is always best to consult an attorney or tax accountant before signing such a contract.

The benefits to such programs are obvious: You may be able to afford a bigger boat than your finances would have allowed if you had purchased the boat on your own; boat insurance may be paid for by management during the period the yacht is being chartered; and maintenance and docking fees may be paid by the company. Though you have to make the boat payment, the charter company pays you a certain percentage of the money the boat earns in charter service, as well as a commission for charters that you book. And, of course, you get to use your boat for a certain number of weeks each year.

The drawbacks: Strangers are using your boat; your time aboard is limited during the duration of the contract; the initial cost of the boat could be more; there are no guarantees that the boat will be chartered; you could end up making full monthly payments; and the boat's resale value could be less than that of a nonchartered boat.

Because each charter management company's terms and contracts are different, you will need to study the contract and pro forma (how they think the boat will perform financially). Have an attorney or accountant look over the contract. Then weigh the advantages and disadvantages, not only financially, but also the intangibles. You will want to compare and weigh such factors as the initial cost, maintenance, potential income and losses, resale value, how you will get the boat from its charter site to your home waters and how you will arrange its sale should you decide not to keep it.

The range of programs and contracts varies widely. Some pay a charter commission as high as 60 percent, but require you to pay part of the boat's upkeep or to carry and pay for insurance. Some require that you keep the boat in charter service for four years; others allow you to take the boat out of charter at any time, usually with thirty days notice. The possibilities are endless, so again, caution is the key.

The Moorings, one of the largest yacht-chartering companies in the world, has a charter program called The Moorings Advantage. Briefly, here's how this company's program works.

Each year, The Moorings buys a certain number of new boats for its world-wide fleet. You buy one of these boats and place it in charter service at one of twenty-three charter bases where it is needed. The charter company maintains, cleans, markets and charters the boat. You get to use the boat four weeks a year (you pay a daily fee to cover fuel and services) and receive a share of the income it generates, which you can use to offset or accelerate the mortgage payments on the boat. The Moorings pays the boat owner 25 percent of the charter and a 15 percent commission for someone you refer who charters for the first time. Other benefits include no dock fees and no insurance payment— The Moorings has its own fleet insurance coverage.

Your initial investment is a down payment (usually 20 to 25 percent of the boat's cost). At the end of the four years, the boat is yours, though not necessarily paid for.

Some charter companies, such as The Moorings, will help deliver the boat to your hometown or offer to sell it for you through one of its brokers. Some companies may charge you a broker commission.

The Moorings also offers a reciprocal agreement that allows you to take a boat equal to yours in size during your allotted weeks at any of its worldwide locations. So if your boat is chartered in Mexico, you can spend two of your weeks in Tonga or the Virgin Islands. However, not every Moorings location participates in this arrangement.

While the boat is purchased from the charter company (already modified for charter service), you must secure financing through a lending institution. Boats modified for charter service typically have more amenities and more cabins to accommodate more people. Most are easily recognizable as charter boats, and the resale values may be lower, despite good maintenance plans; many sailors perceive a charter boat as "overly used" because it stays in constant use. Many classified ads for the type of boats typically used in charter service will carry the message: "Never used in charter service."

Marine lenders typically finance a new boat for fifteen to thirty years, the same length of time as for a house. That's because most new boats cost as much as or more than a house. As sailors are fond of saying, "Owning a sailboat is a way of life, not an investment." Yet many boat owners are able to recoup their investment, and many have made money on the resale.

A BUSINESS PROGRAM

Other companies, such as Bay Yacht Agency in Annapolis, have a slightly different arrangement. Bay Yacht describes its system as a "business program."

Under Bay Yacht's program, an individual buys a boat, finances it for fifteen years and then puts the boat into the hands of the company. All expenses are paid by the company, and the boat owner shares in the revenue.

Bay Yacht estimates that if the boat is chartered for twenty weeks out of the year, the boat owner breaks even. At twenty-nine weeks a year, he realizes a profit. These numbers vary depending on the type of boat (multihulls are more sought after in charter service) and the location (the Caribbean is the most popular).

If the boat owner makes the regular payment and rolls the charter income into extra payments, the boat can be paid for in as little as five years, thus saving interest.

But a boat owner can pull the boat out of charter service at any time. He is not required to keep it in charter for a specified time period. Thirty days notice is required.

Buying a new boat for charter service is expensive. For example, a 38-foot catamaran sells for $125,000 or more. That's why Bay Yacht targets its program at doctors, lawyers and other highly paid professionals.

CHARTER/YACHT MANAGEMENT PROGRAMS

Bay Yacht Agency
Allied/TMM Yacht Charters, 326 First St., Annapolis, MD 21403, (800) 922-4820

Moorings Advantage
19345 U.S. Hwy. 19, N., 4th Floor, Clearwater, FL 34624, (800) 521-1126

Sun Yacht Charters' Management Programs
P.O. Box 737, 59B Union St., Camden, ME 04843, (800) 772-3503

CHAPTER SEVEN

TRAILERABLE, POCKET AND BEGINNER SAILBOATS

"Believe me, my young friend, there is nothing—absolutely nothing—half so much worth doing as simply messing about in boats."
Kenneth Grahame, The Wind in the Willows

No, you really can't put them in your pocket. But these sailboats, also called *trailerable* and *beginner* sailboats, can be taken almost anywhere via land.

In truth, almost any size sailboat can be moved over roads on some type of rig on wheels. But pocket, trailerable or beginner sailboats are the smallest boats of the sailboat world. Trailerable sailboats can be pulled behind a car or truck across the nation's highways.

Boats in this category are seven to twenty-six feet. The smallest ones are used as sailing dinghies, to teach youngsters and novices to sail, and are raced in special "one-design" races. The larger boats in this category are becoming increasingly popular for families and for people who want to scale down, but not give up sailing altogether.

Jerry Correll, whose family owns Trail N Sail, a boat brokerage in New Orleans, Louisiana, that sells MacGregor, Seward and West Wight Potter boats, all trailerable sailboats, finds a wide variety of people are turning to these boats: families with adolescent children looking for a family activity; couples suffering from "empty nest syndrome" looking to take up a new sport; older sailors who have "been there, done that" in terms of a large cruising boat, who now want to enjoy sailing on a smaller, less rigorous scale; and career-oriented people who like to sail but want more mobility.

The smallest boats are sailing dinghies or open boats, those without a cabin or with little space to store things. Sailing dinghies are perfect to put on the deck of a large sailboat to use as transportation or for exploration at a final cruising destination. Or they can be used at the dock or marina for a casual hour or more day sail when you don't feel like taking the "mother ship" out. Most dinghies are made from fiberglass but they may be made from wood. Many sailors who want to try their hand at boatbuilding start with a small sailing dinghy they can make from wood.

As a rule, amenities increase in direct proportion to the boat size. They go from a *pocket*, or cover, for supplies to a small spot to sit when inclement weather approaches, to miniature versions of bigger boats, with a *head* (a toilet), a small *galley* (kitchen) and one or two berths to sleep one or more adults. Most are ingeniously built to incorporate a liveable area. For example, a table may fold down for use and be hooked flat to the wall when not needed. A "sofa," or seating, may be pulled out at night and transformed into a bed.

Pocket sailboats are small, so the initial purchase price is less, new or used. And of course sails, canvas and other amenities are also cheaper. Because they are designed specifically to be put on a trailer, you can easily keep them on shore, in the yard at your house or in the parking lot of your apartment or condominium. That saves money on in-the-water slip rentals, called *wet slips*. Then, when you're ready to sail, you can put them into the water with minimal effort, the same as a small powerboat, using either a private or public boat ramp. The costs of ownership and maintenance put these boats within the financial reach of just about anyone, even children. Consider that a top-of-the-line set of rollerblades and protective gear sells for about $400; a small, used sailboat can be purchased for the same price.

YEARLONG SAILING

In the Northeast and Midwest, where most sailors take their boats out of the water and put them up for the winter, year-round sailing is no longer an option. Not so for the pocket sailor. He simply hitches the trailer to his car, turns on the heater and heads for warmer climes. He can even leave the boat in a sunnier destination for the winter, driving back and forth as time permits to sail.

Those in hurricane- and typhoon-prone areas find pocket sailboats the perfect way to move their boat fast when a storm is approaching.

And people who have limited time to spend cruising find these boats the perfect way to cover large areas in a short period of time. They can depart from home and head for other areas of their state, or cross state boundaries, often in a single weekend. They can return the boat home, or leave it at a new destination on the trailer in a boatyard, with minimal fees compared with leaving it in the water.

ACCESSIBILITY

Pocket sailboats, because of their smaller overall size, have shorter keels than larger sailboats, keels that swing away or that come partially up into a slot in the bottom of the boat. That means being able to go into shallower waters than you can with a larger boat, which in turn means more places to explore once you reach your destination.

The mast is shorter, which means getting under bridges larger boats cannot get under and thus seeing areas not accessible to those in a big boat. It also means not having to wait for bridges to be raised so that you can go under them.

Accessibility to the water is also better, and often cheaper. There are more public and private boat ramps nationwide than there are marinas. Most public ramps do not charge a fee for using the ramp to put your boat into the water, and parking is almost always free. Privately owned marinas usually charge a ramp fee, and perhaps a fee to park your car and trailer. But even if you have to pay to launch your boat, the price is minimal compared with keeping it in the water at a marina. Depending on the area of the country you live in, wet slips range from $.50 a foot to $20 a foot.

LOWER COSTS

How much cheaper is a pocket sailboat? For starters, they range from a few to several thousand dollars for a new or used boat. That compares with $30,000 or more for a new or used boat in the 30-foot and up range.

Of course, used boats can be purchased for much less. How much less depends on a number of factors, including the length, manufacturer, age, condition, and market conditions such as how many are on the market at a given time and how badly the owner wants to sell. But overall, a used pocket sailboat costs less because of supply and demand. These are often "starter" boats, so there are more of them out there. As boat owners move up to a larger boat, they are motivated to sell the smaller one because of the additional cost of owning two boats. Many small-boat owners buy a larger boat and then sell the small one. That makes them even more motivated to sell.

Because many marine service costs are based on the length of the boat (wet and dry slip storage, hauling out and bottom painting are a few), the cost of maintaining a small sailboat is immediately less. This also holds true for major items such as sails (the smaller the sail, the cheaper the price) and for other intangible items, such as your labor to wash and wax the boat; it takes much less time than it does for a larger boat, which means more time spent on the water—the reason you bought the boat in the first place.

THE DRAWBACKS

Pocket sailboats have drawbacks as well. Because the boat is usually kept on a trailer, you must learn to use the trailer, and then there is additional upkeep for the trailer, such as tires and rust prevention. You must learn to tow a boat and trailer, to back up and take turns and to launch the boat at a ramp. Plus, you must have a car or truck capable of pulling the added weight of trailer, boat, people and gear, and may even need to add items such as heavy-duty shock absorbers to a vehicle capable of pulling the weight. You have to put up with traffic jams and other highway-related problems, including flat tires and possible accidents. Moreover, when you finally reach your destination, you'll have to raise the mast, connect the rigging and do other chores before you're ready to sail. When your boat is kept in the water, you simply power out of your slip, assuming you have an auxiliary motor, raise the sails and you're off.

One fellow who owned a trailerable sailboat for many years likened his experience on his 18-foot boat to camping out.

"There's usually not room inside to stand up, and cooking on board filled the cabin with heat and odors, so we cooked hot meals on shore. But that was fun, too."

Other trailerable boat owners have found that doing rudimentary tasks, such as brushing their teeth, requires sitting down. But that didn't deter any of them from enjoying the lifestyle such a boat has to offer.

FOLLOWING THE DREAM

Most people who purchase pocket sailboats have dreams bigger than their pocketbooks. They want to cruise the U.S., seeing the nation's capital, the reefs and sunny beaches of Florida, the bays and estuaries along the Louisiana delta, the sights and sounds of San Francisco Bay, the mighty Mississippi, the metropolises and small towns that sit on the edge of the Great Lakes, and even Mexico and other far-flung places—by water. However, they often lack the time and the money. They can't afford to quit their jobs and take off for a year or more. So trailering a boat becomes a way to fulfill the dream without giving up their stable lives and jobs.

They realize their dreams in several ways: by taking the boat to destinations on weekends and vacations, and then returning it to their home; by leaving the boat at a destination and driving back to that place to continue their voyage; or by taking off for a summer and "driving" the boat from place to place, often crossing the U.S. in the process.

For the latter choices, logistics are often a problem and may lead to increased costs. For example, if you trailer the boat to Louisiana and then sail it over a period of time to Texas, you'll eventually need transportation back to your car.

One pocket sailor looked at that as part of the adventure: He enjoyed taking a bus back to the car. While that can be fun, you have to figure in the costs in terms of fares and time when you opt for that kind of adventuring.

Another pocket sailor solved that dilemma by having her mother join her for the car ride to a destination. The mother didn't like sailing, so she would spend the weekend in a motel or visiting friends and relatives nearby, then pick up her daughter, and the sailboat, at an agreed-upon destination.

Like any boat, owning a pocket sailboat has its tradeoffs. While your friends are spending sixteen hours of a four-day weekend—two whole days—sailing to and from a destination only sixty miles away, you'll be there within two hours and have more time on the water when you get there. And you'll be back home watching the 6 P.M. newscast while they're still battling storms.

 TIP

The cost of some things increases exponentially for boats over twenty-six feet. For example, in Florida, annual boat registration fees are $10 for a boat sixteen feet to less than twenty-six feet, and $51 for a boat twenty-six feet to less than forty feet.

DAY-SAILERS

Day-sailers are categorized as small sailboats in the 12-foot and under range. Most everyone has seen these; they're hard to miss, with their bright, colorful sails, as they scoot across the water.

These are ideal boats for children and for anyone just learning to sail, but don't be fooled by that. Many boats in this size range are raced the world over in "one-design" competitions—boats of the same manufacturer, size and equipment whose skippers are racing against each other, with sailing and racing skills as the hallmark of the prize.

Day-sailers are also called open boats. They tend to be lightweight and can be sailed on small lakes and ponds, and on sheltered rivers and bays. Because they are lightweight, the helm is more responsive, and many people like that closeness between boat and sailor. It also makes them "tender," more apt to heel, but many models have full-flotation hulls, which makes them difficult to sink. In fact, these boats are built so that if they do turn over, they can be easily righted in the water by a child.

The beauty of these boats is that they are the least expensive of all boats. Used models can be bought for as little as $300 and new ones usually are less than $5,000; again, the price varies by manufacturer and size. If you decide to purchase a larger boat for overnight cruises, the day-sailer (if small, seven to eight feet, and lightweight enough) can be used for a dinghy.

Day-sailers will get you into shallow harbors and waterways that you can't normally get to, somewhat like a canoe, but with a sail to contend with. Few of these boats have auxiliary motors; oars are the means for propulsion when the wind dies, or when you want to go exploring with the sails down.

TIP

People who join their boat manufacturer's "fleet organizations" often benefit from group purchases of equipment and have a ready supply of used boats, boat parts and information.

They are easily launched from a waterfront backyard, or hauled on a small trailer to a boat launch anywhere in the U.S. And they can be easily *rigged* (set up) by one person, even a child.

Used day-sailers are advertised in the classified sections of newspapers and marine publications, and on bulletin boards at marinas and marine stores. Also, since many yacht clubs and sailing clubs use these boats for training, it may be possible to pick up a *very* used one cheaply when they are replaced with new ones.

FURTHER READINGS

Brown, Larry. *Frugal Yachting, Family Adventuring in Small Sailboats.* Camden, ME: International Marine, 1994.

Brown, Larry. *Sailing America: A Trailer Sailor's Guide to North America.* Camden, ME: Seven Seas, 1990.

Burges, Robert F. *Handbook of Trailer Sailing.* 2nd. ed. New York: McGraw-Hill, 1992.

TRAILERABLE AND POCKET SAILBOAT BUILDERS

Cape Cod Shipbuilding Co.
7 Narrows Rd., Wareham, MA 02571, (508) 295-3550
  DaySailer

TIP

If your family is divided between a go-fast powerboat and a take-it-easy sailboat, try the MacGregor 26. It can handle a fifty horsepower engine. Dump the water ballast and it reaches speeds of twenty-five knots, fast enough to ski!

Catalina Yachts
21200 Victory Blvd., Woodland Hills, CA 91367, (818) 884-7700
Catalina

Custom Fiberglass Products of Florida
8136 Leo Kidd Ave., Port Richey, FL 34668, (813) 847-5798
Antares, Sovereign, Express Weekender

Doughdish, Inc.
380 Wareham Rd., Marion, MA 02738, (508) 748-0334

Flying Scot, Inc.
157 Cemetery St., Deer Park, MD 21550, (301) 334-4848

Hobie Cat Co.
P.O. Box 1008, Oceanside, CA 92051, (800) 462-4349

Hunter Marine Corp.
P.O. Box 1030, Route 441, Alachua, FL 32615, (800) 771-5556
Hunter

Hutchins Company, Inc.
1195 Knapp Dr., Clearwater, FL 34625, (813) 443-4408
Com-Pac

MacGregor Yacht Corp.
1631 Placentia Ave., Costa Mesa, CA, (714) 642-6830
MacGregor

Menger Boatworks, Inc.
121 Maple Ave., Bayshore, NY 11706, (516) 968-0300
Menger Cat

Nimble Boats, Inc.
6135 142nd Ave., N., Clearwater, FL 34620, (813) 539-6444
Nimble

Nor'Sea Marine
P.O. Box 14, Dana Point, CA 92629, (714) 855-8344
Nor'Sea

Pacific Seacraft Corp.
1301 E. Orangethorpe Ave., Fullerton, CA 92631, (714) 879-1610
Flicka

Pearson Yachts
West Shore Rd., Portsmouth, RI 02871, (401) 683-0100
O'Day

Quickstep, Inc.
17 Broad Common Rd., Bristol, RI 02809, (401) 254-0400
Quickstep

Sunfish Laser, Inc.
P.O. Box 10, Portsmouth, RI 02871, (401) 683-5900
Sunfish, Laser

Vangard Racing Boats
16 Peckham Dr., Bristol, RI 02809, (401) 254-0960
Optimist

West Wight Potter
International Marine, 904 W. Hyde Park Blvd., Inglewood, CA 90302,
(800) 433-4080
West Wight Potter

SMALL BOAT ASSOCIATIONS
Flying Dutchman Class Association
(603) 424-2414

Flying Scott Sailing Association
(803) 765-0860, (800) 445-8629

Laser Class Association
8466 N. Lockwood Ridge Rd., Sarasota, FL 34243, (813) 751-6216

Sunfish Class Association
P.O. Box 128, Drayton Plains, MI 48330, (810) 673-2750

CHAPTER EIGHT

BUYING A USED SAILBOAT AND NEW BOAT BARGAINS

O nce you've decided that sailing and boat ownership are for you, the next step is to determine what kind of boat to buy. Many people start by buying a small boat and then trade up. Depending on your needs, desires, ambition, confidence level and pocketbook, you may want to start with a day-sailer and move up to, say, a 23-footer, then to a 30-footer or larger. Or you may start with a 30-footer and keep that boat for many years. There are boats with one mast, a sloop, two masts, a ketch, among other features, and boats with one, two and three hulls. The decision has everything to do with what you want the boat for. Each choice has advantages and disadvantages. What kind of boat should you consider? Here are some examples.

I JUST WANT TO PUTTER AROUND THE WATER FOR A FEW HOURS.
Buy a day-sailer. The benefits: inexpensive way to sail; boat can easily be stored and moved from place to place on a small trailer; ease of handling and sailing; large selection of used boats; low entry price ($1,000 or less and up). If you tire of the boat or sport, you have little money invested and you're likely to get much of it back. The disadvantages: may take longer to resell; putting it in and out of the water or hauling it to a body of water may become a hassle; the boat usually does not come with an auxiliary engine, so if the wind dies, you may be stuck or have to row; not suited for ocean or rough water sailing (even in a sheltered bay, a storm can suddenly turn a picture-perfect day into a nightmare). Overnight stays may be out of the question unless you take a tent.

TIP

Some states exempt a boat from registration if it is used on a lake or pond, or if the boat is not powered by a motor.

I'M HOOKED ON SAILING AND I WANT A BOAT TO SAIL FOR A FEW HOURS, AS WELL AS ONE THAT I CAN SPEND WEEKENDS AND MAYBE A WEEK OR TWO ON DURING THE SUMMER.

Start with something new or used in the 21- to 30-foot range. Boats that size usually have a small *galley* (kitchen), *head* (portable toilet), cabin with a fold-up table and sleeping accommodations for two to six people. Though the smaller models may be cramped quarters for more than two people, you'll get a lot of mileage from a boat this size. Some people compare a week in a small boat to camping, though the accommodations are more spacious than those afforded by a tent. The drawbacks are that when a boat is twenty-five feet or longer, you'll probably have to keep it in the water at a marina, which means slip fees that vary widely across the U.S. These are called *wet slips*. On the other hand, if you leave the boat in the water you'll benefit from the congeniality of fellow boaters at the dock.

NEW OR USED?

"Looking at bargains from a purely commercial point of view, someone is always cheated, but looked at with the simple eye both seller and buyer always win."

David Grayson, Adventures in Contentment

New boats are expensive, there's no doubt about it. And the bigger they are, the more expensive they become. Yet every year thousands of people buy new boats. They may be buying a dream boat they plan to keep for a lifetime, or they may simply want a boat less apt to break down or need repairs. They may also be able to customize the inside of a new boat to their own specifications. Plus, new boats benefit from years of experience of what works and what doesn't, they may be roomier or they may be built from newer materials using new technology.

If you decide a new boat is for you, there are a few ways to save money. One way is to buy the boat at a major boat show. Boat shows usually offer specials (price discounts) good during the show or for a short period thereafter. Often, however, if you buy a boat at the show at a discount, you may be stuck buying whatever optional equipment is on board, whether you want it or not.

TIP

When buying a new sailboat, have the "extras," such as electronics, dinghy and outboard motor, put on by the manufacturer. You may be able to get them wholesale, and the cost is rolled into the loan. The drawback is that you pay more interest on the loan, because it's larger than it would be with just the cost of the boat.

Another way to save money is to shop around. Brokers buy boats from builders the same way automobile dealers buy cars from manufacturers—cash. They either finance their purchases through a bank at a special lending rate, prime plus 1 percent, or pay cash. The longer the boat sits on their property or in the water, the more it costs them in terms of finance charges, maintenance and dockage. And new models come out each year. Brokers are motivated to sell.

The markup on a new boat is about 25 percent, so there is room to negotiate the asking price. Large brokers may be able to sell a boat for less because their overhead may not be as high as a small broker's, or because they deal in large volumes. Look around long and hard, comparison shopping before you buy. Having the cash to purchase the boat may not be an incentive to discount the price, because the broker doesn't care if the money comes from the bank or you. But if he is in a situation where he doesn't want to wait several weeks or more for the closing, cash could be a great motivator.

BUYING A USED BOAT

Buying a used boat saves you a considerable amount of money compared to buying a new one, and "good deals" can be found from time to time. A boat owner going through a divorce, being transferred to a location where boating

TIP

Your homeowners insurance may provide liability and other coverage for you and your family if you rent, charter or purchase a boat under twenty-six feet. This will spare you the expense of purchasing separate boat insurance. Check with your agent, or read your policy carefully.

TIP

Freedom Yachts has a "fly, try and buy" program that rebates the charter cost if you purchase a Freedom within a month.

isn't feasible, who is ill or who has financial woes will often discount the asking price to make a quick sale. Often such sales are word of mouth and never advertised. That's one good reason to hang around marinas and sailing clubs.

Other places to find a real bargain are popular overseas cruising destinations such as the Panama Canal, the Virgin Islands, the Polynesian Islands and the Caribbean. The reason is simple. Many people are unprepared for what the sea can dish out, and when they reach a destination after a baptism by fire they are adamant about not sailing back. So they sell the boat where it sits, often for much less than it's worth. One veteran cruiser told of reaching the end of the Panama Canal and seeing dozens of boats for sale. One look at the roiling Pacific and its huge waves is often enough to send the not-so-hardy back to sheltered water, and to put their boats on the market.

Often, these are well-equipped cruising boats outfitted for ocean sailing. If the boat is paid for, the owner may have more leeway in selling at a price that is way below the boat's value. If the boat is financed, the owner may even sell it where it sits for the balance owed. That means you will have to fly to the boat's destination and sail it back, a journey that may take months. But the owner benefits from such a sale, becaues she is able to return to a land-based life, doesn't have to worry about someone stealing or damaging the boat or about the boat's safety. And she most certainly will not have to pay dockage and endure the hassle of arranging for it at a location thousands of miles away.

Stateside options abound as well; there are several for buying a good boat at a low price. They range from buying a newer model in good condition when the owner is "motivated" to buying an older model in good condition, to buying an older model that has been neglected but is still fixable. Still another option is to buy a boat seized by the federal government and sold at auction.

TIP

Consider buying a new boat at the end of the model year. Like car dealers, some boat dealers discount "leftover" models.

If you decide on a newer boat in good condition, the price may be high, but you will probably not have to invest much time or work to fix it up. And the cost is certainly lower than buying the boat new. Choose a reputable broker to help find one in your price range that meets your needs. Keep in mind that the broker represents the seller, not the buyer, even though he may spend a lot of time helping you find a boat you want and need.

PRICE VARIABLES

You should be aware that boat prices vary for a number of reasons:

- **Demand**—Following a major hurricane, there be may be fewer good used boats on the market.
- **Geographic Area**—You will probably pay more for a boat in Georgia than for a comparable one in Fort Lauderdale or Annapolis, huge sailing centers with hundreds of boats on the market.
- **Use**—A boat used strictly in fresh water in northern states may command a higher price than one used in salt water in southern states because of the toll sun and salt take on the boat.
- **Condition**—A well-cared-for boat will fetch a higher price than one that has been neglected.
- **Age**—An older model is almost always less than a newer one, but again, some of the factors mentioned above come into play. An important factor is the manufacturer—some boats hold their value no matter how old they are because they are perceived as being built by a quality manufacturer. It's like the difference between a Rolls Royce and a Ford. But like cars and wine, some years are better than others, even among manufacturers. Some sailors swear that the older Morgans are better built than the newer ones. Plus, you need to know if the original builder that was known for building quality boats is still the builder; many builders have changed hands in recent years, or have merged with other companies.

BUY THE BOAT THAT MEETS YOUR NEEDS

The boat you buy should meet your short-term needs and desires. If you dream of sailing the world, but you don't see that as a reality for ten to twenty years, buy the type of boat you will use now. A well-equipped blue-water boat, with heavy-duty fixtures to withstand the rigors of ocean cruising, that is built for the same conditions will cost more than a boat designed to be used in more sheltered waters.

You'll find used boats listed for sale at marine brokers and in the classified sections of newspapers, local, state, regional and national sailboat publications, in sailing club and organization newsletters and magazines, and on bulletin boards at marinas and marine stores. The industry has a book of used-boat prices similar to the one used by the automobile industry. The book for boats is the *BUC Used Boat Price Guide*. The BUC book will give you a wide range of prices representing a particular boat's value. Boats of the same year and builder are hard to compare on paper because of a variety of factors, including upgrades, which may include new electronics or a new engine or new wiring. One boat may be standard, just the way it came from the factory, while another may have had many amenities added over its life, such as heavy-duty rigging, refrigeration, bimini (a cockpit sun shade) and other enclosures. And one boat may be well cared for, while another has been sadly neglected. One may include an expensive dinghy with a motor, another may not have a dinghy. The only way to really compare them is to look at them.

The U.S. Coast Guard has a boating safety hotline you can call for information on boats recalled for safety reasons, and *Practical Sailor*, a magazine about boats similar to *Consumer Reports* (it does not take advertising), does independent surveys of older boats. The magazine also compares and rates the equipment, gear and maintenance items of various manufacturers, including radar reflectors, outboard motors, bottom paint, varnish and hull wax, by durability and cost. It will often recommend a cheaper model or item that works as well as a higher priced one.

Remember, too, when shopping for a used boat the price plus repairs you put into it still may not exceed the boat's replacement value—what it would cost you to buy a similar boat today. For example, an older model, 40-foot boat valued at $55,000, even if it needed $20,000 in repairs, could not be replaced today for less than $200,000 new.

SHOPPING FOR A USED BOAT

Your best used-boat buy may come from a private owner. The price may be lower because the boat owner doesn't have to factor in the broker's commission, on average 10 percent of the sale. But that's not always the case. If the owner is in financial distress, has already purchased a larger boat and is paying dock rent on both boats, is going through a divorce or is recently widowed, you may get the boat at a real bargain price.

Buying a used, older boat that has been well maintained can be an excellent choice for a small investment. Mass-produced fiberglass boats have proven themselves for over thirty years now. However, you'll have to put up with some inevitable imperfections, such as *crazing*, spidery cracks in the gel coat topsides, and perhaps dull and yellowed gel coat on the outer layer. But there

TIP

If you have your heart set on a boat and the seller won't budge on the asking price, the broker may take less of a commission in order to make the sale. The difference in his commission would be deducted from the seller's purchase price.

are products on the market that can put a shine on older boats. And cosmetics should not be your main concern—seaworthiness should be. As long as the hull is structurally sound, you can live with the cosmetic imperfections.

An older boat in poor condition may be had at a bargain price, but rehabilitating it may be more than you bargained for. Marine supplies are expensive, and the task that looks easy usually isn't. One broken fixture may lead to several others, until you're spending all your time at the dock fixing and no time sailing. When that happens, you may curse the day you bought it. But if you're handy with mechanics, woodworking and other boat chores, you may find such a project an enjoyable challenge. Wood, steel and ferrocement boats are generally less expensive and easier to repair than fiberglass.

In general, boats built and sold in Florida usually cost about 20 percent less than in other parts of the country. The reason? Economics. In the Northeast and on the West Coast, wages are higher, corporate taxes are higher and, in fact, almost everything is higher. That means the cost of manufacturing a boat is higher. In the South, especially in Florida, these same economic indicators are very low. So a boat manufacturer in Florida can sell its boat for less than, say, one in New York.

The same goes for used boats, but for different reasons. Wages and dockage are lower in Florida than in the rest of the nation. That means it costs less to repair, maintain and keep a boat in the Sunshine State. That's good to keep in mind, too, if you need boat repair work done.

TIP

Some insurance companies will not insure a boat over twenty years old; those that will usually require a survey. If you are buying a boat more than twenty years old and it's in less than prime condition, check before you sign on the dotted line to ensure that the boat is insurable.

TIP

The percentage paid a broker to sell a boat is negotiable.
Discounts are most common on very expensive boats, but if
a broker is hungry, he may accept less.

RESOURCES

Booth, W.D. *Upgrading & Refurbishing the Older Fiberglass Sailboat.*
Centreville, MD: Cornell Maritime, 1985.

Mustin, Henry C., *Surveying Fiberglass Sailboats: A Step-By-Step Guide for
Buyers and Owners.* Camden, ME: International Marine, 1994.

U.S. Coast Guard Boating Safety Hot Line
(800) 368-5647

A LESSON IN INGENUITY

Noah D. White was twenty-two years old when he dreamed of owning and
living aboard a boat. But the cost of a new or used boat in the length he was
seeking made the quest fruitless. Plus, he would have to work for years to put
aside enough money for the down payment.

He did what many in his position have done: bought a "junk" boat, one
that was salvageable only for the value of the hull. White bought a 1966
Cascade 42 for $2,500 cash plus $1,200 worth of labor to pay off a lien the
owner owed the boatyard. In good condition, the boat is worth between
$50,000 and $60,000.

At first, he thought he could salvage the wood superstructure, but he found
it was rotted throughout. Living aboard, in near-primitive conditions, he began
tearing down the wood to the fiberglass hull and began the slow task of rebuilding. A year and a half later, he had nearly half-finished the project, and invested
about $900 in materials, not including tools and supplies. How? He explains:
"Dumpster diving. I check the dumpsters at marinas and boatyards every
night."

From one high-end boatbuilder's dumpster, he regularly gets large and
small pieces of teak and mahogany. Other sailors and friends who have fol-
lowed his journey with interest and sympathy keep on the alert for bargains.
Some examples: A shop teacher at a local high school brought him yards of
fifty-year-old seasoned Douglas fir planks, which had been the school's

bleacher seats before they were torn down. Another friend bought a warehouse and its contents, and found gallons of marine paint and adhesive in it. For $50, he bought $1,800 worth of awlgrip and adhesive.

He plans to take the boat to Fort Lauderdale next year because "they have richer dumpsters" and better used-boat equipment stores and flea markets.

"I thought it would cost me about $30,000 to fix it up," White says, "but so far, I'm spending about one-fifth of what I expected to pay."

GET A SURVEY

Before you sign on the dotted line to buy your used boat, have the boat checked from bow to stern, inside and out, by a surveyor. A boat surveyor represents the buyer, not the seller, and his services are arranged for and paid for by the buyer.

Most boat sales contracts contain provisions that the purchase is subject to survey and *sea trials*, a test sail. Be sure that these two items are included as part of the sales agreement, if they're not already in the contract.

Unless you're an expert on boats, and few people are, it is nearly impossible to detect all the problems that a boat can hide. A good survey is necessary, and a good surveyor will have the boat hauled out of the water so that the bottom hull and keel can be checked as well.

The surveyor will spend at least eight hours in and around the boat checking everything from water tanks to the engine, sails, wiring, hull integrity, keel integrity, the rudder and everything in between. He also should use an instrument to check the hull on fiberglass boats for moisture, which creates blisters.

The surveyor will tell you what's good and what's bad about the boat. He may recommend things that should be repaired before you buy, preferably at the seller's expense. And if you follow behind him during his inspection, you'll learn much you will need to know about the boat.

Moreover, your boat insurance company and lending institution will want to see the survey before they provide insurance or lend you money—to protect their investment as well as yours.

The written survey will give you more bargaining power on the asking price, too. If the surveyor finds minor or major problems with the boat, get an estimate of the cost to repair and/or replace the problem items and reduce the asking price by that amount. Or see that problems are fixed before you buy the boat.

Surveyors usually charge a flat rate based on the length of the boat, on average about $10 a foot. So the cost to survey a 40-foot boat would be about $400, money that is well spent.

But surveyors are not created equal. Most states do not require surveyors to be licensed. A national organization of surveyors has been formed, but the group is not licensed by a government body. Remember, however, that even members of organizations can be honest or not. For example, one man said he paid a surveyor who was a member of the surveyor's association $200 in exchange for valuing the boat at the price needed to refinance it. The survey, done while the boat was in the water, took only three hours for a 38-foot boat.

As with many situations regarding sailboats, word of mouth is the best way to get the skinny on things. Ask friends and other sailors who they would recommend to do a survey. And ask about the surveyor's credentials and other boats he has surveyed.

BUYING DAMAGED BOATS

Buying a boat damaged by fire, sinking or a hurricane from insurance companies can be an inexpensive way to buy a boat you might not otherwise afford. When a major hurricane strikes, such as Hugo in North Carolina or Andrew in south Florida, a great many boats are damaged. Insurance companies often "total" a boat that can be fixed because of the high costs associated with repairing the boat, or because the yards are inundated with storm-damaged boats and the waiting list for repairs may be months. They may also sell a boat that can be repaired because the owner refuses to have it repaired and wants it "totaled" instead. Insurance companies then sell the damaged boats at distressed prices. How much you can save depends on many factors, including the number of damaged boats, the number of buyers and the extent of the damage. In general, a fixable, high-quality boat can be bought for about 40 percent of its value in good condition. If that sounds like a good deal, it is, but beware. There are no guarantees on such boat purchases, and you must know a lot about repairing boats or have the time and patience to learn. You will need to find one that has not suffered damage to the hull's integrity. Repairs can be costly even if you are able to do the work yourself, because of the high cost of materials: fiberglass, paint, gel coat, stainless steel fixtures and rigging.

But if you are handy with boat repairs and have the time to devote to such a project, you can save a considerable amount of money and get a boat you might never be able to afford otherwise. A man in California bought a fire-damaged boat worth $75,000 for $10,000.

Dennis Buyer, of Jacksonville, Florida, bought a 42-foot Pearson valued between $75,000 and $85,000 then—and now—for about $30,000 at an auction after Hugo ripped through the Carolinas. He attended an auction held by three insurance companies in Charleston and successfully bid on the boat. Opening bids started at $25,000. After paying cash (banks seldom finance damaged boats), he put out another $1,500 or so to have a crane hoist the boat onto a trailer and to pay a company to transport the boat to Jacksonville.

Four years and about $25,000 later, the Buyers are enjoying their boat. Buyer makes several points worth noting: He had the skills to do all of the work himself, enjoys doing the work, and stored the boat on his own property, thus saving on labor and storage rental space. Many marinas will not allow boat owners to do major projects at the dock.

Buyer also did serious upgrades on the boat, rebuilding it to last a lifetime. A perfectionist, he admits that 50 percent of the work, the costs, and the time spent on the project were not hurricane-related damage.

In hindsight, "I'm glad I did it," he says. "I can't recommend a hurricane damaged boat to anyone else, because so much can go wrong."

FINDING A DAMAGED BOAT

Ernie Bratts, a claims adjuster for BOAT/U.S., says most insurance companies will take the names of people who are willing to buy damaged boats. Most opportunities do occur after a hurricane. As soon as a major hurricane makes landfall, call insurance companies and ask to be put on the buyer's list. Each company has its own rules and schedules. BOAT/U.S. operates this way: It takes the names of interested buyers and sends them a list of boats to be sold and the auction date. It then puts all the boats in a staging area where potential buyers can look them over. It usually takes closed, sealed bids and sells to the highest bidder. Payment, via personal check or bank draft, is usually required within a few days.

Some companies sell the boats where they lie, in the marsh, on top of docks or half sunk in the water, and the buyer agrees to remove the boat from where it is. Some hire a professional auctioneer, and others use a variety of bidding systems.

Depending on the damage, value and worth, boats may sell for $50 or $70,000. In general, a higher quality boat will command a higher price than a cheaper model (sort of like the difference between buying a wrecked Mercedes-Benz or a Chevrolet Cavalier). Bratts says sometimes a boat is not too severely damaged to repair, but the boat owner refuses to have it fixed. The insurance company will sell a boat under those circumstances as well, perhaps selling one that can be fixed for $60,000 for $40,000.

Boats damaged by fire, sinking or other catastrophes can be purchased from insurance companies. Fewer of these boats will be repairable; those that can are generally repaired by the insurance companies. Still, it pays to put your name on an insurance company's list. You never know what may come up.

BANK REPOSSESSIONS

Another way to buy a used boat cheaply is to look for bank repossessions. When a boat owner defaults on his payment to the lending institution, the bank or finance company wants to get rid of the boat quickly. These companies are not in the boat-owning business and don't want to pay the cost of keeping the boat at a dock or in dry storage, not to mention the cost of insurance on the vessel. So they sell the boat, usually for the balance owed, which often is considerably less than the boat is worth.

A woman in California bought a 36-foot cruising sailboat valued at $29,500 for $12,500 under such conditions.

However, finding such deals isn't that easy. Lending institutions typically have agreements with local boatyards or brokers to purchase such boats, and the boatyard then fixes the boat, if needed, and sells it for its market value.

Your best bet is to keep your ears and eyes open. But call marine lenders—banks and credit unions—in your area and ask to be put on their list to buy repossessed boats. Having a particular size or type of boat in mind may be helpful.

AUCTIONS

Several branches of the federal government hold regular auctions of boats they have seized for a number of reasons, among them drug trafficking and nonpayment of income taxes.

Boats seized for drugs may be heavily damaged, because they have been torn apart to search for concealed drugs. They often can prove burdensome to the new owners, even after they are repaired. If the new boat is boarded, the scent of drugs may still be present and drug dogs may indicate drugs are on the boat when they're not. People who purchase such boats need careful documentation about its previous "life," but even so, owning such a boat can result in a lot of hassle.

The U.S. Coast Guard and U.S. Customs turn over their confiscated boats for auction to a company to sell for them. Check with the U.S. Customs office in your area to find out which company sells the boats. Call the company and ask to be put on its auction notification list.

Boat auction companies are becoming more commonplace. These companies sell demonstration boats and trade-ins for builders and manufacturers, or they sell boats seized by the U.S. Marshall, U.S. Customs or other government agencies. They may contract with lending institutions to sell repossessed boats.

Shop these very-used boats carefully. Many have been neglected or abused. Most auction companies will allow you to have a boat surveyed before you purchase it.

Auction companies will mail or fax a list of boats coming up for auction to you. In general, only about 10 to 20 percent of the boats auctioned are sailboats. Some also charge a bid fee of $20. On average, these boats sell for 10 to 20 percent below the lowest BUC value.

You can also check with state and local marine law enforcement agencies. These agencies will usually have annual auctions of goods confiscated, and they may have an occasional sailboat.

BOAT LIQUIDATORS AND AUCTIONS

Asset Recovery and Liquidation Specialists, L.C.
(303) 584-7041

EG&G Dynatrend
(305) 621-2306
Miami, Florida, company that auctions boats for U.S. Customs and the U.S. Coast Guard.

International Boat and Marine Auction Services
(800) 530-4561
Offices in Florida, Arizona, South Carolina and Nova Scotia. Auctions government-seized boats on a regular basis, and represents boat manufacturers.

National Liquidators
(800) 633-7172
Bank repos, weekly sealed-bid auction.

ABANDONED BOATS

Marinas and anchorages are the places to find boats abandoned by their owners. In most cases, these boats are paid for and, for a variety of reasons, the owners have simply abandoned them. This was more common with the old wooden boats than it is today. Perhaps the owner fell upon hard times and couldn't pay the slip rental; or perhaps the boat needed repairs that the owner couldn't afford. The reasons people abandon boats are numerous, but that doesn't help marinas that are stuck with someone else's problems.

Federal, state and/or local marine laws govern such abandoned property. In some areas, the boats cannot be sold or disposed of readily. In other areas, they can be sold only under certain conditions. When the marina is able to legally sell the boat, it often does so for whatever it thinks the boat is worth, or for what a buyer is willing to pay. Most sales take place years after the boat is abandoned, and often such boats require serious repairs. At other times, the repairs may simply be cosmetic.

One young man in Washington, DC, came upon such a deal. He bought an abandoned 22-foot Pearson Electra from a marina for $500 and spent a year restoring it, relying on junked boats, used sailboat parts, discount sails and his own labor. The boat had been neglected for about ten years, but it was in good shape. When he finished, he had invested a total of about $1,200, including the purchase price. The boat was worth at least $3,000 when he sold it for much less because he was moving to another state.

BUYING FROM A NONPROFIT ORGANIZATION

Some nonprofit organizations, usually those that are marine related, take boats as donations for their own use or to resell them. The donor gets a tax-deductible contribution for doing this. If the organization is marine related, it may use the boats for projects, or it may sell the boats and use the money for another worthy endeavor.

Such nonprofit organizations are an excellent place to find a used boat at a price well below its market value.

For example, the Maritime and Seafood Industry Museum in Biloxi, Mississippi, operates this way, according to Director Robin Krohn. It advertises for individuals and corporations to donate boats to the museum. When the donor calls, the museum evaluates the boat. If it's salable, the owner must obtain an appraisal. Then the museum offers a price based on the appraisal. The donor gets to write the amount of the donation off his income tax as a charitable donation. Meanwhile, the museum either decides to keep the boat for its fleet (it has two schooners and a skiff used in its sailing program), advertises the purchased donor boat for sale or asks for bids on it, usually for a price much less than its true market value. A museum committee decides which bidder, usually the highest, gets the boat.

"We may accept a bid of $2,000 for a boat worth $4,500," says Krohn. "That's 50 percent of the appraised value. They can get boats much cheaper from us because we're trying to turn them over quickly. Everyone wins. We get the money to fund our operations, the buyer gets a boat at a bargain price and the donor gets a tax donation."

The quantity and quality of donated boats vary. Some may be powerboats and others may be sailboats. They could be small skiffs or yachts. Krohn says the museum sold a motor yacht last year for $70,000, though it was worth much more. And a neighboring program, the YMCA in Ocean Springs, recently had two cigarette boats, worth $80,000 each, donated.

"We're new to this and small," Krohn says. "Museums on the East Coast have many more boats than we do."

Depending on the income tax bracket that a donor is in, the donation could amount to a significant tax savings.

Many nonprofit organizations and museums seek boat donations and buyers by advertising in sailing magazines and newspapers, and sometimes in daily newspapers. Call and ask to be put on an auction or buyer's notification list.

Alexandria Seaport Foundation
Jones Point Park, 1000 S. Lee St., Alexandria, VA 22314

Christian Enterprise
(800) 846-1341

D'Var Institute
(800) 338-6724

Maritime and Seafood Industry Museum
115 First St., Biloxi, MS 39533, (601) 435-6320

Mystic Seaport Museum
Mystic, CT 06355-0990, (860) 572-0711

Philadelphia City Sail
Rick LeFevre, (215) 951-0330

CHAPTER NINE

BUILDING YOUR OWN

Another way to put yourself behind the helm of a sailboat is to build one—or at least part of it. Some well-known yacht designers sell their boat plans, and a number of companies sell plans and instructions for do-it-yourself kits. Boats that you can build yourself range in size from an 8-foot sailing dinghy to a 40-foot or larger yacht. These boats may be built from wood, steel, fiberglass or *ferrocement*, an extremely popular building material in the 1960s and 1970s, especially in California. But again, as with buying and rehabilitating a boat, you need to have some skills and the time and money to put into such a project.

Though many plans and kits contain enough step-by-step information to construct a boat, you probably will need to learn new skills to perform the work, despite claims that "anyone can do it." Some can, some can't. You will have to buy a few special tools as well.

WOODEN BOATS

Plans and kits for wooden boats may be geared toward beginners, and often will say so. For example the "tack and tape" or "instant" method of building a wooden boat is the easiest for beginners who have little or no woodworking experience. If you dream of building a large boat, you might start with a small sailing dinghy, using this method.

Laminated-wood construction and similar methods require intermediate woodworking skills; the plank-on-frame method requires advanced carpentry skills and tools.

Gaining boatbuilding skills isn't all that difficult. For instance, many waterfront communities have nonprofit organizations and museums offering courses in small wooden boat building. Prices for these courses are nominal, and help is readily available every step of the way.

For example, the North Carolina Maritime Museum in Beaufort, North Carolina, offers year-round courses in boatbuilding carpentry. The museum is close to the Intracoastal Waterway, so cruising sailors often extend their stay to attend a course. Skill-building courses cost between $60 and $80, while a hands-on course where you actually build a boat is about $350. The prerequisite for the latter course is an introductory course where basic skills are taught. Most classes are small, six to eight students, so personal attention and help are almost guaranteed.

The Center for Wooden Boats in Seattle, Washington, attracts "wannabe" boatbuilders from all over the U.S. They spend a week or two of their vacation time building or restoring boats, or perhaps working on a group boatbuilding project. Most courses range between $350 and $450. The nonprofit center also has a foundry class that teaches people to make bronze parts for wooden boats; bronze boat parts are difficult to find.

FIBERGLASS AND STEEL BOATBUILDING

Some colleges, high schools and trade schools offer courses in steel or fiberglass boatbuilding. A person who teaches such skills may be willing to tutor you, out of a love of teaching or for a fee.

Fiberglass can be tricky to work with, but the skills required are easily mastered. Protective clothing and a mask are necessary. Fiberglass materials are expensive, but they are also forgiving, so if you make a mistake, it can often be corrected easily.

Steel is not as difficult for beginners to work with, and the skills for working with it are fairly easy to learn. But you may need a large, covered area to work in. On the plus side, steel costs less than other boatbuilding materials.

BUYING A HULL AND DECK

Still another option is to buy the hull and deck from the boatbuilder and finish the inside yourself. Or to build the hull and deck and have someone else do the inside.

Do-it-yourselfers estimate that about 25 to 30 percent of the cost of the boat is in the construction of the hull. So if you buy the hull and do the rest yourself, you'll save more money and spend less time building.

Ed and Becky Morgan of Atlanta, Georgia, bought a used boat whose interior had been completed by its owner. In the early years, the company that made the 28-foot Bristol Channel Cutter sold only the hull and deck of its boats. The one the Morgans bought had been made in 1976, but didn't make it to the water until 1983. They found it in Bellingham, Washington.

Though in fair condition, they wanted to make it a showpiece like others in its class. After paying $45,000 for the boat, Ed spent seventeen hundred man-hours and $20,000 rebuilding the interior, which included new plumbing and wiring.

Because they were on a limited budget, the Morgans found a number of unique ways to save money on purchases (several of these are listed in chapter 12).

Nor'Sea, a well-known, respected and established boatbuilder in California, gives buyers an option. They can buy a 27-foot boat ready to sail for about $80,000, or one of two kits.

One kit only requires the interior to be finished, saving the buyer about $20,000. The company estimates that interior work can be accomplished in about five months. The other kit, of which few are sold, is just the deck and hull. The builder estimates that option requires about five years to complete, but the savings are about 50 percent over the cost of the ready-to-sail model. The savings come in labor, valued at $20 an hour.

Nor'Sea builds about eight boats a year, and has sold about fifty kit boats in the seventeen years it has been in business.

Dennis Buyer, the fellow who bought the hurricane-damaged boat, learned some of his boatbuilding skills by completing a hull-and-deck kit. He bought the hull and deck of a 30-foot boat from the manufacturer and finished it himself.

"There are so many excellent hulls and decks to buy, I would never build one from scratch," Buyer says. "Plus, from the first day, you're working on finishing it rather than on starting it."

But was it a good investment? Not really, according to Buyer. His total cost for buying the hull and deck and finishing the boat himself was $30,000, about what he would have paid at the time for the finished boat. He sold it for $17,000.

DO IT FOR LOVE, NOT TO SAVE MONEY

Building your own sailboat brings immense satisfaction, but it may not save you as much money as you might think. How much you save will depend on the type of boat, the size, the material and your ability to do all of the work yourself.

Drawbacks include spending years, perhaps, on the shore, building, instead of being out on the water, sailing. The amount of money saved may not be significant compared to buying a used or new boat. Factors to weigh on the plus side include saving finance charges on a boat loan and knowing the boat intimately.

Greg Delezynski of Powder Springs, Georgia, spent five years building a sailboat that was fifteen feet long on deck. He started the project while living in Los Angeles in 1988 and finished it just before moving to Georgia in 1993. The $10 plans from a reputable firm said he could build the boat for about

$800. He kept copious notes of his progress and costs. In 1995, he had spent $2,362.22 and still had modifications that would make the boat sail better. A new boat would have sold for about $2,000 in 1988.

In fairness, Greg admits he went overboard, using better materials than the plans called for. For example, if the plans called for screws, he bought brass ones at three times the cost of stainless steel. Instead of using the recommended glue, he used expensive epoxy.

"Build a boat for the right reasons," cautions Delezynski, "because you want to build one, not to save money."

He has since built an 8-foot mahogany sailing dinghy that took about six months to build and cost about $600, just as the plans predicted.

And he purchased a 1978 27-foot boat to fix up, "so that I could have something to sail."

Greg says he spent a lot of time in California in boatyards taking to people who were building boats from 10 to 110 feet. Over the years, he found that less than 10 percent ever get finished and to the water. And the ones that do get finished and to the water never go cruising, because the owners have spent so much time, energy and money in the building.

The other drawback to building your own boat is that they are tough, if not impossible, to resell. The builder knows how well it is put together, but the buyer has no such guarantees. On the other hand, since such boats are difficult to sell, they may be very inexpensive to buy. Again, buyer beware!

FINAL THOUGHT
PLACE A COIN AT THE MAST STEP

Even today, sailors continue with this age-old tradition of good fortune, whose roots are steeped in superstition. The custom of placing a coin or coins at the heel of the mast (or masts) ensured there was money to pay the fares of the crew across the River Styx if the ship should be lost at sea. Coins must be placed face up to avoid disaster. Hiding a coin somewhere on board, with the location, date and value known only to the owner, enables the owner to prove the boat is his.

BOAT PLANS AND KITS

B&B Yacht Designs
P.O. Box 206C, Vandermere, NC 28587, (919) 745-4793

Boat Plans, Inc.
P.O. Box 18000, Boulder, CO 80308, (800) 782-7218

Bruce Roberts Designs
P.O. Box 1086, Severna Park, MD 21146, (410) 544-8228

Clark Craft
16 Aqua Lane, Tonawanda, NY 14150

Conser Catamaran
1995 Irvine Ave., Costa Mesa, CA 92627, (714) 645-0272

Glen-L Marine Designs
9152 Rosecrans, P.O. Box 1804, Bellflower, CA 90706, (310) 630-6258

Ken Hankinson Associates
P.O. Box 272-C, Hayden Lake, ID 83835, (208) 772-5547

Nor'Sea Yachts
P.O. Box 14, Dana Point, CA 92629, (714) 489-8227

BOATBUILDING CLASSES
The Center for Wooden Boats
1010 Valley St., Seattle, WA 98109, (206) 624-3028

North Carolina Maritime Museum
Beaufort, NC, (919) 728-7317

WORLDWIDE WEB SITES
E-mail: jmertens@bbs.mpcs.com
   Boat plans and technical information-sharing forum for boatbuilders. Open discussions by amateurs, yacht designers, builders and professionals.

A Boat Builder's Place
The Sea Chest
   Stuart Wier's List—List of resources for boatbuilders.
   website: http://www.efn.org/~jkohnen/nautical.html

RESOURCES
The Benford Design Group. "Small Craft Plans: 15 Complete Designs for Dinghies and Tenders." Drawings and plans for building wood boats.

Buchanan, George. *Boat Repair Manual.* Houston, TX: Gulf Publishing, 1992. All types of boats.

Hankinson, Ken. *Fiberglass Boat Building for Amateurs.* Bellflower, CA: Glen L. Marine Design, 1982.

Klingle, Gilbert with revision by Thomas Colvin. *Boat Building With Steel. 2nd. ed.* Camden, ME: International Marine, 1973.

Self, Charles. *Woodworker's Source Book. 2nd ed.* Cincinnati: Betterway Books, 1995. Hundreds of listings of manufacturers, mail-order sources, courses and associations.

CHAPTER TEN

SWAPPING AND TRADING

S wapping is a great way to sail for free in another part of the country. The concept is simple. A boat owner in one part of the country, perhaps Maine, swaps time on his boat with a boat owner in another part of the country, say Florida. Most of these are tit-for-tat deals, a week on your boat for a week on mine.

Or the swap may involve time in one person's house, condominium or apartment for an identical length of time on another person's cruising, live-aboard yacht.

And the trade may even be a waterfront house for a waterfront house. One advertisement offered a five-acre island with a cottage on a "famous lake in Ontario, Canada" for time in an oceanfront cottage in the Florida Keys or the Bahamas.

As you can imagine, many such swaps allow snow-weary Northerners to escape to warmer climates during winter. And those in hot spots like Miami, Florida, or Texas will look to the north for relief during the hot summers.

Such swaps may be a one-time deal or an ongoing yearly exchange. You may enjoy sailing Washington every year, or opt for diversity by swapping with different people in different parts of the country. The key to either deal is that it must be fair and balanced. You wouldn't want to swap the use of your million dollar home for a dilapidated 25-foot sailboat.

Such exchanges are infrequently advertised. Usually they result from meeting an individual with whom you are compatible and arranging the deal spontaneously. When swaps are advertised, you will find them in classified ads under Wanted or Boats For Sale Or Trade.

Wanted: To exchange time with well found [capable] sailing yacht 35'–40' located in FL/Islands, winter, for same located New England summer. Extensive experience.

Either way, you will need to be cautious. After determining that a match is likely, here is a checklist of things you should do:

- Ask for personal references.
- Exchange photographs and descriptions of the domicile or vessel to be exchanged.
- Consider asking for a security deposit to cover possible damages.
- Consider drawing up a formal agreement that spells out the rights and responsibilities of each party.
- Check with your home or boat insurer to ensure you are adequately covered and that such an exchange will be covered.

A book editor in New York regularly trades two weeks a year on her 34-foot Hunter for equal time on an identical boat berthed in Fort Lauderdale. She and her husband met the other couple at a Hunter sail-in and hit it off. One night during a get-together, the New York couple were talking about how nice it would be to spend part of the bitter northeast winters in a sunny clime, and the Florida couple echoed those sentiments—in reverse. They had dreamed of sailing in the northeast during the summer when their children were out of school, but didn't have the time necessary to take off for months for the trip, nor the money to charter a boat for two weeks. Why, they asked each other, can't we trade? They have been trading now for three years, without a formal agreement, and the arrangement has worked out fine. In fact, they have become close friends. Their rules are simple: Leave the boat the way you found it, and minor damages are paid for by the party who did the damage.

If you do decide on a formal agreement, here are some things you should include in the contract:

- Dates and time period covered
- Description of the property or vessel and accessories, if applicable
- House or boat rules
- Maximum number of people allowed
- Policy for guests
- Who pays for what damages, when and how
- Procedures for loss or theft of valuables

Those who exchange homes and boats should also provide a list of emergency contact numbers and information on how various equipment works. Though most sailboats basically operate the same way, each has its own quirks. For example, the outboard engine may start perfectly when handled a certain way that only you are aware of (don't give it gas at first, pull the choke, pull the starter twice, and as soon as it starts, turn off the choke and give it gas), or the garbage disposal in your sink at home may not accept pieces of food larger than a certain size, or may be subject to jamming. Relaying such information not only avoids problems and possible repair bills, but also makes for a more pleasant vacation and one worth repeating. Following are some suggestions for your list.

HOUSES

- Special instructions for appliances or for machinery such as swimming pool filtration systems
- Names of friends or relatives who may call and what to tell them
- Emergency telephone numbers: police, fire, rescue, water and electric companies
- Garbage and/or recyclable pickup days
- Instructions for operating heating and cooling systems

BOATS

- Special instructions for operating "ornery" equipment
- Instructions for taking on fuel and water
- Instructions for operation and location of all safety equipment and gear, including VHF radios, fire extinguishers, halogen systems, flares, man-overboard poles and retrieval systems, radar, LORAN, abandon-ship bag, first-aid kit and SATNAV
- Location of through-hull fittings
- Instructions for operating head and stove

Of course, other things can be added to either list and those will depend on the type and size of the boat or house and the experience of the sailors.

TRADING

Another way to swap is to make a permanent trade. Such trades can be boat for boat, a smaller boat for a larger boat plus cash, or a house for a boat and vice versa. One sailor was even offered an antique car in exchange for his boat.

A boat-for-house trade can work well for people who sell their house and worldly goods to cruise the world, and years later want to trade in the sailing life for that of a landlubber. If they have been gone for a number of years, they may have all of their money tied up in the boat, and may not want to wait to sell it before buying a house. Or they may have to reestablish credit before a bank will loan them the money for a house. In such instances, a trade may work when a direct sale won't. Conversely, qualifying for a boat loan can take some doing, as boats are still considered luxury items by lenders. So someone with a modest home and income may not qualify for a boat loan, and may be willing to trade her home for the boat she desires to take cruising. Trading is just another form of creative financing.

Needless to say, such swaps are limited only by the seller's and buyer's imaginations and willingness to trade. You will find such requests in the classified sections of sailing magazines and newspapers.

Some advertisers will be specific about what they want to trade, say a boat valued at $150,000 for a house of equal value in the Bahamas. Others will leave the door open by saying "all reasonable offers considered."

A man in Texas advertised a trade for his "luxury home in Houston" for another person's unused sailboat through a boat broker. The broker explained that the man was an experienced sailor and racer who was looking for a boat to cruise for a year or more. The house was an unoccupied rental property.

"It's fairly unusual," the broker said of the trade. More common are people who want to trade a smaller boat plus cash for a larger one, thus limiting their cash outlay and getting rid of the second boat simultaneously.

"Boats aren't like cars," he notes, "where the dealer buys a trade-in and then resells it. When you're talking about a $100,000 boat, a dealer can't afford to do it. But if you have a $100,000 boat to sell, you might take $70,000 for it, and a smaller boat worth $30,000 in trade. Then you can turn around and sell the smaller boat."

Another reason to trade is change of lifestyle. As cruisers age, they may find the rigors of caring for a large boat no longer to their liking. Yet they may want to continue sailing on a smaller boat. Then they may opt to "trade down," exchanging the large cruiser for a day-sailer or trailerable sailboat. Depending on the worth of each boat in the trade, one party may also owe the other party money. This works well when the party with the larger boat is looking for a smaller boat, and the party with the small boat is looking for a cruiser.

Some examples of ads for trades are:

Exchange/Sell 30' Chapparel Signature. Too fast for older owner. Will swap for condo (with dock) Middle/Upper Keys or SW Florida coast.

Retiring from boating? Principal will trade an inherited 2br/2ba single-family condo on a golf course in FL for a trawler or motor yacht of equal value (60K). Can add some cash.

Trading may have income tax and other tax implications as well. If you decide to make a trade, you would be wise to consult a tax attorney or accountant; they may add to the following list of possible tax liabilities, which vary depending on your own financial situation. These variables reflect the differences in income tax brackets and subsequent taxes, age and other factors.

HOUSE

• Homestead exemption—Some states offer a homestead exemption (a reduction of ad valorem taxes for making the house your principal home) under certain circumstances. Usually there are residency requirements, such as a specific time period and the month in which you purchased the house. The current owner may have these exemptions, but you may not for a certain period of time.

• Capital gains—At this writing, the capital gains tax was still in effect, which means if you sell your house, you have to pay a tax on the portion of the sale that is over the original cost of the house plus improvements. The law presently allows a once-in-a-lifetime rollover of the capital gain for either spouse. The rollover clause states that you are exempt from the capital gains tax on the principal residence you have lived in for at least three of the last five years if you are age fifty-five or older and put the money earned from the sale into another residence within a certain number of years.

• Income-producing property—Income-producing property always has income tax implications that should be thoroughly checked, including capital gains adjustments for deductions taken over the life of the property as a rental.

• Foreign governments—If you plan on swapping for property in a foreign country, including the Bahamas and the Virgin Islands, you may have to pay extra taxes because you are not a citizen, or you may be subject to a higher duty on imported goods, including your own household goods. This can increase the cost of ownership.

BOAT

• State taxes—Most states require that a buyer pay state sales tax on a boat purchase, even if the tax was already paid by the previous owner in the same state. And some states require you pay tangible property taxes on a boat. Also, you may have to pay dual state sales tax, to your own state and the state where you purchased the boat, or you may have to pay state sales tax to your state and a "user fee" to the state where you purchased it.

When you strike a deal, or negotiate a preliminary deal, make sure you have a contract. The contract should spell out everything, including recourse should anything not be up to par. A minimal contract should include:

• The "sale" price of both properties (boat and car, house, etc.)
• Basis of value (average of two appraisals, one appraisal, etc.)
• Amount of cash to be paid by buyer or seller

- When cash must be paid to buyer or seller
- Terms of owner-held loan and interest rate (The IRS requires that market-rate interest be paid on any loan. It usually accepts prime plus two percentage points.)
  - Terms of the sale (such as pending sea trials)
  - Any warranties
  - Protection against ship or property liens

CHAPTER ELEVEN

SAVING ON GEAR

"Of all the fabricks, a ship is the most excellent, requiring more art in building, rigging, sayling, trimming, defending, and mooring, with such a number of severall termes and names in continual motion, not understood of any landsman, as none would think of, but some few that know them."

Captain John Smith

A s with everyone else, sailors like to save money. But cruising sailors and those building or renovating a boat are especially good at it. Those who quit their jobs to sail for months and years at a time have a vested interest in continuing their chosen lifestyle, and that means saving as much money as they can along the way, especially for gear. People of limited means who are working on project boats have money-saving systems down pat.

Both groups know where and how to get the best prices on new and used sails, fittings, rigging, books and charts. Even then, if the price is not within their reach, they resort to other means, ranging from raiding dumpsters to ferreting out free dockage. Because they often need products in the far corners of the world where, in some countries, you cannot buy goods even if you have the money, they've learned to adapt and pre-plan.

But that's not to say that they have all the secrets. Most sailors find ways to save money on gear. And there are many: discount marine stores, mail-order catalogs, consignment shops, liquidators and surplus marine stores, and flea markets. They also trade, barter and even raid garbage cans.

DISCOUNT MARINE STORES

Is there a state in the union with a sailable body of water that *doesn't* have a discount marine store? Chances are slim. Being a "discounter" is much in vogue in the savvy 1990s, but not all stores who claim to be discounters are; some items may be discounted only a little, some not at all. But true discount stores do exist. Do your homework and comparison shop. That's the only way you will really know if you are saving money.

Some discount marine stores offer savings in the 10 percent range on most merchandise, and as much as 30 percent for some sale items. Some are national chains; others are owned by individuals. An individually owned marine store may not call itself a discounter, but may nonetheless have prices below those of a nearby "discounter." The price you pay at any store is based on a number of business variables: cost of overhead, operating incomes, wholesale prices paid and competition. An independently owned store off the beaten track may have small rent payments for the building, whereas a major chain may take expensive space in a mall. The savings in rent could be enough for the independent to make up for the loss of not being able to buy wholesale by volume, which chains benefit from and which leaves independents more vulnerable costwise. In areas where there is a large cluster of marine stores, prices may be lower than in areas where there are only a few. In competitive areas, many marine stores will match the others' prices, sometimes even if it's a sale item.

TIP

If you are doing extensive boat work, incorporate your project. As a company, you can buy products wholesale from manufacturers.

An independent may also be a "hybrid" store that sells gear on consignment or buys the inventory of failed stores. That's where the bargains really begin. On the other hand, an independent's prices may be considerably higher than a nearby chain, but service and knowledgeable salespeople may be its forte. Or, like one independent marine store in Florida, the owner may have had the business, and part of the stock, for several decades so that hard-to-find parts are readily available.

DISCOUNT STORES

Aegis Marine
1602 Monrovia Ave., Newport Beach, CA 92663, (800) 747-3014
New gear, much of it at below discount prices.

Boat Builders and Sailors
Sixteenth St., Costa Mesa, CA 92626, (714) 548-9619
Housed in an airplane hanger. Publishes a catalog; new gear, deep discounts.

BOAT/U.S.
880 S. Pickett St., Alexandria, VA 22304, (703) 823-9550

Challenger Sailcloth
104 E. Main St., P.O. Box 716, Vernon, CT 06066, (800) 962-4499
and
Challenge West
711 W. Seventeenth St., E-4, Costa Mesa, CA 92627, (800) 423-6750
   Both stores sell brass and plated marine quality hardware. Will send a free catalog.

E&B Discount Marine
201 Meadow Rd., Edison, NJ 08818, (800) 533-5007

Fawcett Boat Supplies, Inc.
110 Compromise St., Annapolis, MD 21403, (410) 267-8681
   Publishes 545-page catalog, in color where needed (paint). Savings of 15 to 25 percent on hardware and 25 to 40 percent on paint.

H&L Marine Woodwork, Inc.
2965 E. Harcourt, Rancho Dominguez, CA 90221, (213) 636-1718
   Good prices on wood and other products.

Ocean Electronics
P.O. Box 90, Buford, GA 30519, (404) 798-7857
   Sells 600-foot spools of half-inch, three-strand twist nylon for $129. Other bulk bargains available.

West Marine
500 Westridge Dr., P.O. Box 50050, Watsonville, CA 95077, (800) 538-0775

SALVAGE, SURPLUS AND CONSIGNMENT STORES

Discount store savings pale in comparison with the savings you may find elsewhere, at marine flea markets, liquidators and used-boat supply stores. How do you find them? Ask around. Most are word of mouth; such stores seldom advertise. Occasionally they may advertise in local sailing newspapers or in the classified sections of large consumer publications, but not often. The good ones usually don't have to advertise; some do just to keep their name in front of the sailing public.

   The primary difference—other than price—between discounters and the other options is merchandise availability. If you need a part and need it now, price isn't important and retailers are the place to go. But if it's a luxury item, "toy" or backup piece of equipment you are searching for, you will want to look around for the best price. Before you buy used gear there are other things to consider and ask: Is it refundable or exchangeable if it doesn't fit? Does it work?

Some discounters and used-equipment stores specialize in one item, the most famous of which may be Bacon & Associates in Annapolis, Maryland, which specializes in sails, in addition to used gear. Many a cruiser will say, "Every sailor knows about Bacons" but those new to sailing usually do not.

Some marine stores set aside a portion of their space for consignment goods. A sailor brings in an item he wants to sell, say a marine stove, and sets his price. The store adds a markup, usually 10 to 20 percent, and that becomes the asking price. Often the price is negotiable, though the store may have to check with the seller to see if he will take the lower price. Many times he will.

Salvage stores buy less-than-perfect goods from manufacturers, usually goods that are scratched or dented. They also buy parts, such as winches and cleats, from individuals or companies that salvage parts from old boats destined to be sunk or demolished.

These stores often offer some of the best buys around. Savings ranging from 50 to 80 percent off the retail price are common in true marine salvage stores.

Some salvage stores stick to a particular product, such as engines or sails. Bacon & Associates of Annapolis, Maryland, in business for thirty-eight years, has more than ten thousand sails—for dinghies to maxiboats, new and used—in its huge warehouse.

The company takes sails on consignment from individuals going from racing to cruising or vice versa, it buys sails from manufacturers that have repossessed sails from retailers, it acquires sails from retailers and sail lofts whose customers didn't like the final product, and it takes the inventory of failed boatbuilders.

"It's everything from much-used to new," the company says. Bacon catalogs its sails by size and boat type, so a customer can call from anywhere in the country and give either the size he is seeking, or the size, type and model of boat, and get a list of all the sails that fit the category. Typically, the list will include information such as weight, material, manufacturer, whether it has slides, reefs or sail numbers, and the condition of the sails, along with the price.

A number of sail shops now mimic Bacon's successful formula; they often advertise in the classified sections of sailing publications.

Some of these stores will pay cash for your used gear. If you are short on money or want cash from something old to pay for something new, you might consider such a deal. But like selling to a pawnshop, you probably won't get the highest price.

One last note about used gear. Some builders and manufacturers are beginning to get in on the craze, too. For example, Hinckley Yachts, builders of very beautiful and expensive sailboats, now sell used masts to the public. Check with the manufacturer of your boat to see if similar buys can be found, and keep your eyes peeled for such bargains in sailing publications' classified sections.

SAILOR-RECOMMENDED USED AND SURPLUS STORES

ATK Marine Engines
(800) 421-3746
　　Remanufactured, imported and domestic engines.

Bacon & Associates
116 Legion Ave., Annapolis, MD 21401, (410) 263-4880
　　Ten thousand new and used sails in stock.

Fawcett Boat Supplies, Inc.
110 Compromise St., Annapolis, MD 21401, (800) 456-9151
　　Sailboat parts and accessories, wholesale. Sells to the public; free catalog.

Hinckley Yachts
(207) 244-5572
　　Used and refurbished masts.

Jamestown Distributors
28 Narraganset Ave., P.O. Box 348, Jamestown, RI 02835, (800) 423-0030
and
Hwy. 17 and 21, Gradens Corner, Rt. 1, P.O. Box 375, Seabrook, SC 29940
　　Boatbuilding and woodworking supplies and fasteners, free catalog, U.S. and Canada.

Minney's Ship Chandlery
2537 W. Coast Highway, Newport Beach, CA 92663, (714) 548-4192
　　Surplus and used gear.

The Nautical Trader
110 E. Colonial Lane, Nokomis, FL 34275, (941) 488-0766
　　Buy, sell, trade, consign and surplus.

Newport Nautical Supply
186 Kalbfaus Rd., Newport, RI 02840-1309, (401) 847-3933
    Consignment shop, manufacturer's close-outs. New and used products.

Old Lyme Marina
(860) 434-1272
    Refurbished crankshaft kits.

Sail Exchange
407 Fullerton Ave., Newport Beach, CA 92663, (800) 628-8152
    Buys and sells used sails. Savings of up to 70 percent.

Sail Warehouse
(800) 495-7245
    Used and surplus sails.

Sailorman
350 E. State Rd. 84, Ft. Lauderdale, FL 33316, (305) 522-6716
    Free catalog of new and used marine hardware.

MAIL ORDER

Mail order came to boating many years ago and continues to flourish. Mail-order houses usually offer gear at lower-than-retail prices because they don't have to pay overhead for store fronts—but their prices may not always be the lowest, especially if you have to pay taxes and shipping charges. The key to saving is knowing what things cost. Finding out is easily accomplished by comparing prices with other marine stores and catalogs.

Here are some key questions to ask: How much is postage and handling, and who pays for it? If the item has to be returned, who pays for postage? Does it have to be in the original carton? Do you need prior approval to return it? Who pays for the long-distance call? What about service and support?

Sometimes when you add in these factors, the mail-order price may not be a bargain after all. And you may have to wait a few days to receive it, as most mail-order houses ship products in the least expensive way. If you want it overnight, you often have to pay extra for that service.

Yet for expensive or hard-to-find products, mail order may prove to be just the ticket.

Some of the larger, better-known mail-order companies have opened retail stores all over the country, but there may still be a discount available when you use the mail-order side. Most of the discount marine stores listed under the retail store heading also have mail-order service. A number of retailers now have mail-order catalogs as well. Ask.

NAUTICAL FLEA MARKETS

Nearly every sailing community holds a nautical or marine flea market sometime during the year. The "swap meet" may be held the same time each year, and may be sponsored by a sailing club or organization, marina or marine store.

The Dania Marine Flea Market in Dania, Florida, lays claim to being the largest outdoor flea market in the nation. Each April for the past eighteen years, thousands of sailors converge on the Dania jai alai fronton to pick over the wares of hundreds of vendors—retailers, manufacturers, liquidators and individuals. The cost for spectators is $5 a day; vendors rent space. The flea market has become so successful that a new contender is setting up shop in Tampa, Florida, in 1996. The Tampa Nautical Exchange and Marine Flea Market is set for February each year at Tampa Stadium. This flea market is expected to draw up to 250 marine dealers and antique traders, as well as public vendors.

At marine flea markets you'll find sailors who have held on to gear and equipment they no longer want or need and are now ready to sell. Sailors may put off buying nonessential items and wait for such annual sales. Quite often, individuals buy as much as they sell.

Some sellers make a living purchasing the inventory of defunct or bankrupt marine stores or marine manufacturers and reselling the gear at such enterprising marketplaces for a fraction of their original retail price or market value. Large and small marine retailers may also see such flea markets as a way to rid themselves of old and unsold inventory that doesn't sell in the store. As always, let the buyer beware!

Dania Marine Flea Market
Al Behrendt Enterprises, 499 E. Sheridan St., Suite 317, Dania, FL 33004, (800) 275-2260

Tampa Nautical Exchange and Marine Flea Market
Tampa Stadium, (813) 724-3201

 TIP
Marine and other manufacturers may let you buy direct from them at wholesale, or at discounted retail prices. Ask.

TIP

Take a magnet with you when you shop for hardware. Many allegedly stainless steel and brass parts aren't, or they are poor quality. If a magnet sticks to brass, it's plated, and not solid brass. Also, a magnet will not stick to stainless steel. When working on the boat, use a magnetic screwdriver. If the "stainless steel" screw sticks to the screwdriver, throw it away—it's not stainless steel.

BUYING NONMARINE SUPPLIES

A few smart sailors have learned that the word *marine* generally translates to *expensive*. They often check nonmarine stores for same-quality items at a lesser price.

One small discount marine store owner found he could save his customers money by checking the catalogs of recreational vehicle wholesalers. He found many of the same items—down to the same part number—sold in wholesale RV catalogs for 30 to 50 percent less than in marine wholesale catalogs. Boats and recreational vehicles have some things in common; for instance, both have DC power systems (powered by battery) and similar sanitation devices.

While sailors must be careful about buying some items that way (boats are built with materials that withstand saltwater corrosion), some things don't make a big difference, like DC replacement bulbs for overhead lights or toilet paper that dissolves easily. Such items are less expensive when purchased from an RV store or supplier than from a marine store.

Other things, like stainless steel or copper fittings, screws, washers and the like, can be purchased from hardware stores at a fraction of the cost of the same or similar items sold in marine stores. Ditto electrical supplies, paints, epoxies and solvents. One sailor wrote to a marine manufacturer of paints and epoxies for the chemical contents of a very expensive marine epoxy he was using. With the information in hand, he was able to find a similar, and

TIP

Buy awning and canvas supplies and tools through a tent and awning or upholstery company and save 30 percent or more off marine retail prices.

 TIP

Dealers and manufacturers often deeply discount new products at boat shows.

---

sometimes even the same, product in another industry at a significantly lower cost.

I can vouch for the durability of Levolor venetian blinds on a sailboat. We looked at custom marine blinds for our 40-foot Morgan Pilothouse, but found them way out of our budget. I went to Home Depot and ordered the blinds I wanted in the color and dimensions that would fit our decor and windows. Using them in a marine environment voided the warranty but, ten years later, they're no worse for the wear and tear that cruising the islands and living onboard a sailboat brought.

Dave Porter discovered a nonmarine alternative to the Sun Shower, a marine product made of plastic that is filled with water and heated by the sun for quick, freshwater rinse-offs. Though not expensive to buy, he found water (a precious commodity at sea and in some countries) was still wasted that way. Porter buys a new one- to five-gallon garden sprayer, paints it black and fills it with water. The sun easily warms the plastic container, which holds the heat for several hours. The spray is pressure driven by pumping air into the container and can be regulated for a hard or soft stream. He bathes in the ocean using Joy liquid soap (sailors' choice because it continues to suds in salt water) and then rinses off. He also finds it handy for rinsing dishes washed in salt water.

NONMARINE BARGAINS

DETCO, Sterling Paints
604 Chestnut St., Conway, AZ 72032-5404, (501) 329-6965

Chemicals and allied products manufacturer. Its paint division makes linear polyurethane paints and two-part varnishes. Wholesale and retail.

 TIP

Go in with friends or dock neighbors to buy line, chain and other such items in bulk. Split the goods and the price accordingly.

TIP
You can buy closed-cell foam for cockpit cushions directly from mattress manufacturers. Many will even custom make a mattress to fit a V-berth or narrow-quarter berths.

DUMPSTER DIVING

Many a savvy sailor has gone to the marina dumpster to empty his trash and found something he could use or needed that someone else had discarded. It might be line, rigging or an old stove that could be easily repaired.

For some real goodies, the dumpsters of boatbuilders are often filled with scrap pieces of expensive teak and other exotic woods. Usually the pieces are small, but not too small for a simple project, such as a mount for winches or trim for a repair job. Many sailors restoring a boat have relied almost exclusively on dumpsters.

Marinas and boatyards that accommodate expensive yachts, those in the quarter-million and up range, offer some of the best pickings. Often, a perfectly good piece of equipment is discarded when the owner upgrades it for the newest model with more bells and whistles. And perfectly usable items like line and sails are often discarded on a "regular maintenance" basis. Some sailors hold on to others' discards as backups for emergencies; some use them to replace their even more-worn items. Others fix them up and take them to flea markets, a way to earn cash and fuel the cruising kitty.

BOOKS AND CHARTS

"I had already found that it was not good to be alone, and so I made companionship with what there was around me, sometimes with the universe and sometimes with my own insignificant self; but my books were always my friends, let fail all else."
Joshua Slocum, Sailing Alone Around the World

Most sailors will argue that books *and* charts are both necessities aboard a well-equipped cruising boat. They may well be.

Charts are necessary everywhere you sail, including your own local area, because they provide water depths, bottom conditions, location of shoals, rocks and other hazards, the height of overhead cables and much more information essential to navigation and sailing. Charts are expensive, not singularly, but because you need so many of them. At about $14 each for NOAA charts, those provided by the National Oceanic and Atmospheric Administration, the cost adds up. For example, on a cruise from one end of Florida to the other, you may need twenty charts or more, depending on whether you want to sail down the Intracoastal Waterway, offshore in the Atlantic Ocean or a combination of both.

If you've already joined the twenty-first century and have a computer on board, and perhaps a navigation system that interfaces with the computer and the boat's systems, you can save money on charts by buying them on CD-ROM. You'll also save lots of room that would have been taken up by hundreds of charts. Resolution Mapping, Inc., of Lexington, Massachusetts, is one of several companies that sell charts this way. For instance, three hundred charts that cover an area from Maine to Florida are available on just one CD-ROM. You can purchase only what you need, maybe the charts for one or two states, or the whole set of charts. You receive the disk with all the charts on it, but you are given the security code only for the ones you have purchased. The cost is $250 for the first ten charts purchased, and $11 for each one after that. If you buy all three hundred charts, a discounted price of $2,475 works out to about $8.25 a chart, compared to NOAA's paper charts at $14.95 each.

The company also offers chart updates from the U.S. Coast Guard notices to mariners. Although these notices are free from the government agency, each change has to be added to the chart it belongs on. For $75 a year, Resolution Mapping will provide the changes on a disk that can be loaded onto the hard drive and updated to the CD-ROM charts. The first time you sign up for this service, the cost is $125, which includes an initiation fee.

The obvious drawback to computerized charts is that if you lose power, you lose your charts. The company expects to come out with a version in 1996 in which the charts can be printed out from your computer. That way, you can have backup paper charts just in case.

Other sources of navigation help come from waterway and cruising guides, which usually cover a given area, like the Florida Keys, the San Juan Islands or the entire state of Florida. A few cover large territories, such as the East Coast Intracoastal Waterway or the Bahamas' 3,000-plus islands. While many of these guides provide helpful sketches and reduced-size charts, they are *no* substitute for real charts. Use them as one more aid.

One way to save on charts is to buy chart books, usually available for a given area, say the Bahamas, the Chesapeake or Seattle areas. Though less expensive than buying individual charts, these books are still expensive, $50 and up.

Frugal chart buyers also look beyond traditional retailers. For starters, swap with a fellow sailor or friend, or borrow them. Advertise to buy someone's used or never-used charts. Some sailors buy charts for areas they plan to visit, but never do. Or they go to an area once and never plan to return, so they sell the charts at a fraction of the cost.

Some government entities provide free charts of areas under their jurisdiction. For example, the Wisconsin Department of Natural Resources offers free charts and guides to fishing and boating on the Mississippi River. You only have to write to the department to receive them.

Boating associations and clubs may also produce free or nominally priced guides to waterways. BOAT/U.S. has a number of free publications available to its members.

Sailing magazines and newspapers also contain classified ads from sailors who want to buy, sell or swap charts, another good way to find them. And some organizations, such as the Seven Seas Cruising Club, have a regular chart-trading center for members.

Books on sailing and marine topics are obtained in much the same manner, through swaps and trades. But books are more readily found along the way in your travels. For instance, most marinas, especially those along heavily traveled cruising waterways, have lending libraries or trading libraries. Usually the rules are simple: Take a book, leave a book. Used book stores in towns along the waterways are good places to find nautical books. Even library book sales will yield books on nautical subjects.

Then there are new and used book stores that cater to mariners. Like marine stores, some sell books on consignment. A few have large mail-order houses.

Also, some marine publishing companies will sell to you direct, and even provide a list of the books that they print. But usually there are no real savings buying books that way.

 TIP
Many sailors buy brand-name outboard motors in the Bahamas because they cost less there than they do in the States, even with the duty charge.

BOOKS AND CHARTS
Armchair Sailor
546 Highway 98E, Destin, FL 32541, (800) 451-4185
website: http://eightsea.com/eightseas/armchair/armchair.html
New and used books.

TIP
Build your own dinghy davits from stainless steel tubing and save a hundred dollars or more.

Bluewater Books & Charts
1481 S.E. Seventeenth St., Fort Lauderdale, FL 33316, (800) 942-2583

More than thirty-five thousand nautical books and charts in stock. Offers thrity-day money-back guarantee. Not a best buy, but everything you want or need.

Columbia Trading
504 Main St., W. Barnstable, MA 02668, (508) 362-8966

Free catalog of new, used and out-of-print books.

International Marine
(800) 882-8158

Marine books, free catalog, direct mail order.

Nautical Book Club
F&W Publications, Inc., 1507 Dana Ave., Cincinnati, OH 45207, (513) 531-2222

CHARTS
Bellingham Chart Printers
P.O. Box 1728C, Friday Harbor, WA 98250

Offers worldwide charts; 20 percent off DMA and NOS originals with twenty-five-chart minimum. Claims chart savings of 70 percent or more.

The Binnacle
15 Purcell's Cove Rd., Halifax, NS B3N 1R2, Canada, (800) 665-6464

Charts of Canada, Nova Scotia and the Arctic.

TIP
If you need a metal part replaced and can't find the replacement for it, see if a local machine shop can replicate it.

TIP

Don't throw old dock shoes away.
Have them resoled.

Resolution Mapping, Inc.
35 Hartwell Ave., Lexington, MA 02173, (617) 860-0430
Charts on CD-ROM.

FREE CHARTS AND GUIDES

Boat/U.S. offers free publications to its members: "New Boat Warranties Guide," "Hurricane Warning Bulletin," "Consumer Protection Guide," "Boating Safety for Kids," "Trailering Safety Tips" and "Weather Watch Pocket Guide."

"Fishing and Boating on the Mississippi River"
Wisconsin DNR, P.O. Box 7921, Madison, WI 53707

Contains safety information, navigation tips, information on locks and dams, and maps of twenty-two river sections with boat access points. Covers the Mississippi from Prescott, Wisconsin, to Dubuque, Iowa.

"1996 Special Notice to Mariners"
Seventh Coast Guard District, 909 S.E. First Ave., Miami, FL 33131-3050

112-page book, navigational information, aids to navigation, first aid.

Note: This covers areas under this Coast Guard Group's jurisdiction. Check with the Coast Guard Group in your area to see if it offers a similar publication.

CHAPTER TWELVE

SAVING ON SERVICES

L ike marine products and gear, marine services can dent the budget in a hurry. Though hourly rates are more in line with those you are accustomed to paying for nonmarine services, it's no consolation when you have to lay down your hard-earned dollars.

Sometimes it seems as if you tend to use more marine services than land-type services, but that's because boats are unique in their sizes and interiors. For example, *biminis*, cloth stretched on stainless steel tubes that covers the cockpit, protecting sailors from rain and sun, are mostly custom made. Canvas covers for winches, boxes and other gear also range greatly in size, requiring each to be made separately. Ditto dodgers, curtains and cockpit cushions.

And, of course, if you can't repair an outboard or diesel engine, or install, repair or replace electrical wiring and rigging, you have to pay someone to do it for you.

TIP

Hourly rates for labor typically are cheaper in southern states than in northern states.

Self-reliant cruising sailors are the ones who stay gone the longest. They know how to make or repair sails, to clean diesel-engine injectors and to clear fuel lines and strainers. They are masters of *jury-rig*, making do when parts are not available at sea or abroad.

Learning how to do boat repairs and projects yourself not only saves you money, but also gives you practical, invaluable experience if you ever decide to chuck it all and go cruising. The smartest sailors find ways to learn how to repair things inexpensively.

And if all else fails, smart sailors often fall back on the age-proven monetary system of bartering for goods and services.

DOCKAGE

Whether land-based at a marina or cruising on a waterway, dockage can eat into your budget. In most parts of the country dockage is reasonable and affordable; in other parts it's already at such a high premium that some boaters must keep their boats on moorings, or purchase a dock space (called a *dockominium*).

For monthly dockage, bargains abound in small towns and cities off the beaten path. In Florida, where dockage rates vary widely by location, sailors in large cities like Miami and Fort Lauderdale may keep their boat in a smaller city within a twenty-mile radius from their own because rates are cheaper. Or they may opt for a smaller, older marina with wooden docks instead of the expensive new one with floating docks.

The Okeechobee Waterway, which connects the west and east coasts of Florida, offers some real bargains in dockage. In between the populated cities on either end are small towns where dockage can be had for $50 a month, or $.50 a foot. Storage can be in the water or on land, and the beauty of this location is that, from the middle, it's only a day's sail to either coast. Many sailors from Europe have learned this and keep their boats there from season to season.

Private waterfront homes are also a good choice for low rentals. People who live on the water sometimes have docks that they don't use, or that they are willing to share for a price far below what area marinas offer.

You might also look for ads for someone seeking a caretaker for a waterfront home, and be able to tie up your boat at the dock free of charge. Or, as one woman did, exchange a weekly check on her house while she was gone for a summer for free dockage.

Look for ads in the classified sections of newspapers or sailing magazines.

While cruising, look for small, out-of-the-way marinas that charge less than large ones. Some state and municipal marinas have very low rates, and some federal and state parks offer free dockage for a night or two. Some small towns

 TIP

If you plan to have your boat moved cross-country by a professional boat hauler, see if you can "piggyback" with another boat headed the same way. One sailor saved hundreds of dollars by shipping his sailboat with a powerboat headed to Florida from California.

provide free dockage, and even free water and sometimes electricity for one or more nights, although usually there is a limit to their generosity.

The City of Port Lavaca, Texas, offers two days' free dockage to visiting boats that have never stayed at the marina before if the skipper says she is a *Mid-Gulf Sailing* magazine reader. Even if you're not, or don't know about the offer (and you know now), the city-owned and -operated marina only charges $2 per linear foot a month, or $5 a day dockage. Port Lavaca is a town of about eleven thousand, about twenty miles from the Gulf of Mexico and just off a large ship channel south of Victoria.

Restaurants, ship's stores and other retail stores that are on the water may offer free overnight docking to patrons. If you don't see a sign, ask.

DOCKOMINIUM

A dockominium works much like a condominium, except that it may not be as good an investment. Deep-water slips have been known to silt in, with the water depth going from ten feet to four feet in a matter of years. And environmental regulations may forbid dredging, or it may be such a costly endeavor that it's not worth the price.

The marine environment is a harsh one, and weather and marine life, not to mention sun, can turn your investment into a costly expense. Hurricanes, tornados and winter storms can wreck pilings and wash away finger piers and docks. Barnacles and worms can eat away at wood pilings. The sun can dry and splinter wood docks. So before you plunk money down for a dockominium, investigate the management, the facility and the environment, as well as government regulations.

Like real estate, dockominium prices vary by location and demand. Deals can be had under similar circumstances: death, divorce, lack of demand, lack of cash or a boat sale. Shop around and keep your eyes open.

DOCKOMINIUM CHECKLIST

• Location—Easily accessible to your home or to an area you like to sail in. Decent neighborhood to help deter theft. Accessibility to ocean inlets and deep-water channels.

• Water depth—Deep enough for your present boat and/or to accommodate a larger boat in the future, or to better your chances for resale, plus several extra feet to cover silting and shoaling over the years.

• Check with Army Corps of Engineers and/or local water management groups to determine if area is progressively silting or deepening.

• Check with federal and state departments of natural resources to learn about environmental regulations and restrictions on the property and terms of submerged land lease(s).

- Construction—Docks, pilings and finger piers should be sturdy enough to withstand severe storms. Plastic or concrete pilings and/or floating docks are less expensive to maintain.

- Amenities—Pump out station, laundry/toilet facilities and work area.

- Management—Personnel should be marine knowledgeable. Company or owner's association should be financially stable and/or have solid business background. Check with Better Business Bureau, Credit Bureau or Securities and Exchange Commission if the company is public, and ask to see 10K and other financial documents.

- Documents—Pro forma will estimate common expenses of owners over a period of years. Read fine print concerning individual liabilities carefully.

BRINGING DOWN THE COST OF LABOR

Even if you have to pay someone to perform work for you, consider these means of bringing down the cost: Supply the materials you have bought used or through a wholesaler, saving the markup the service provider charges on goods; offer to help the service person in exchange for a lower hourly rate (you will also learn more by doing this); offer the use of your tools, if you have them and they need them; see if a marine employee will agree to do the work freelance on Sunday or a holiday; and offer to pick up any needed parts or supplies.

Better yet, have the work done at a nonmarine facility, when applicable. Ed Morgan of Atlanta, Georgia, who refinished a boat, saved $700 by having his mast painted at a car body shop instead of a marine boatyard that specialized in masts and rigging. Another sailor hired a crack automobile and truck diesel-engine mechanic to fix his boat's engine when the boatyard's mechanic couldn't find the problem. The savings on labor were considerable and the work was done correctly the first time.

If you use your imagination, you are sure to find other ways to save on

 TIP

When you need canvas work done (biminis, dodgers and sun covers), see if you can save money by providing the cloth yourself.

services by using nonmarine service providers. But again, be careful. Non-industry laborers may not know anything about marine requirements and codes.

DO IT YOURSELF

Self-reliance can derive from need, as well as the satisfaction of doing the work yourself. Whether it's the necessity of repairing an inboard or outboard engine at sea, or simply learning how to make your own sails, there's immense satisfaction in facing a problem and providing the solution. This is what makes cruising sailors an independent lot. Those who aren't either have a lot of money or don't race, sail or cruise for long.

Learning new skills isn't difficult; teachers abound. For starters, try "experts" in your sailing community who often are willing to help you with a project, from rebuilding the engine to sewing canvas covers or sails. The expert may be someone who does such work for a living, or who has picked up the skills by doing it himself and likes to share his knowledge. Most sailors fall in the latter category.

TIP

Purchase a Necci heavy-duty sewing machine for $200. It will sew through five layers of canvas and is much cheaper than a marine-grade sewing machine.

If that fails, there are hundreds of do-it-yourself books for sailors, some good, some fair. Such books can show you how to repair gel coat and other boat fixtures, how to make items from wood for your boat or how to sew boat cushions. Manufacturer's manuals are also good resources for learning how to do the job yourself. Even if you're not handy with repairs, manuals can help you troubleshoot the problem. In doing so, you may find that an adjustment, which you can easily do yourself, instead of a repair may be all that is needed.

For instance, one sailor had constant problems with his radar unit—everything was at a 45° angle. After taking it into the shop to be checked out and paying a service fee, he learned that it only needed resetting, which the owner's manual pointed out. Had he read the manual before rushing to the repair shop, he would have been able to make the adjustment himself and save money.

Many sailors have also learned to make things for about half the price of ready-made. Stainless steel dinghy davits are easily made by novices and the savings are considerable. Other projects include teak plate and cup holders and other teak interior fixtures, as well as upholstering seat cushions.

COMMUNITY COURSES

If you want hands-on training, most communities, especially those near large bodies of water, have a number of resources for continuing education courses on a range of subjects. These resources may include colleges, universities, sailing organizations and clubs. In Jacksonville, Florida, the community college has a marine industries school on the river. If you sign up for its course on marine inboard engines, you can bring your boat to the school's dock (for a small fee) and work on your engine as your class project. That way you not only learn engine repair, you learn it for your own engine on your own boat: handy information when you're hundreds of miles offshore.

Do-it-yourself sailors estimate that they knock off about 60 percent of the cost of a repair or project by doing the work themselves. Of course, some things may be too difficult or too complex for you to handle, so you may want to pay someone to do those, and save the do-it-yourself work for simpler undertakings.

Some of the most simple projects to learn from books and manuals are rope splicing, sailmaking and small-engine repairs. For the mechanically inclined, diesel-engine repair and other shipboard systems installation and repairs will be fairly easy if you have a good manual or instructions. Sailmaking requires more room than in-depth knowledge.

INSURANCE

Boat insurance is costly and, in areas hard hit by hurricanes in the past few years, it's difficult to obtain. But if you have financed your boat, your lender most likely will require that you keep it insured.

Most long-distance cruisers whose boats are paid for take the risk and don't carry insurance on their vessels. One cruiser said that he figures out the annual cost of insurance on the boat, and then spends that amount each year on safety features.

There are a few ways to save on insurance, according to Rick Cote, an agent with Shoreline Insurance Agency, Inc., of Clinton, Connecticut. Shoreline is an independent insurance brokerage that shops an average of thirteen insurance companies to get the best buy for its clients.

 TIP

A table band saw is about the same price as a good quality jigsaw and can do much of the same work and more.

One way some boaters seek to save on insurance is to increase the deductible, but Cote says that's not always wise. With the average cost of a boat falling somewhere in the neighborhood of $120,000, a 1 percent deductible comes to about $1,200; at 2 percent it's $2,400, and the savings is only about 5 percent. But if you need to cut corners somewhere, that 5 percent savings may come in handy.

Insurance companies base their ratings on several factors, and the best rates go to those who have years of sailing under their belts, who have taken courses on safety, who have a boat well-equipped with navigation gear (LORAN, GPS) and who have previously owned a boat. Insurance for sailboats is about 40 percent less than for powerboats.

Liability accounts for about 10 percent of the premium; the rest is for the hull.

"It's foolish to buy boat insurance without liability," says Cote. "You can live with damage to the boat, but if there's bodily injury and someone sues you for $1 million, it doesn't go away."

If you live aboard your boat, getting insurance may be slightly more difficult—some insurance companies won't insure you, or the premium will be more expensive. Luckily, not all insurers feel that way. Some even specialize in insurance for those who choose to live on their boats. Check around and compare prices before you buy.

 TIP

Save on haul-outs by buying scuba equipment, or use an air hose.

BOAT INSURERS

Acordia/Pettit-Morry Co.
520 Pike St., 20th Floor, Seattle, WA 98101-4095
　Yacht insurance exclusively for liveaboards.

BOAT/U.S. Insurance
880 S. Pickett St., Arlington, VA 22304, (703) 823-9550

J. Everett Eaves, Inc.
650 Poydras, Suite 1500, New Orleans, LA 70130

Shoreline Insurance Agency, Inc.
250 E. Main St., Clinton, CT 06413, (800) 762-7462

BARTERING

When you are in a bind because you can't afford to have something fixed, or you are away from the mainland and its services, you might consider bartering. If you can repair an outboard engine with ease, but can't repair a bimini or a cockpit covering, you could exchange your expertise for someone else's. Most cruising sailors get along fine that way, but the trade doesn't have to be a service for a service. Some don't even consider such trades bartering. Many a sailor has asked someone on the dock for help with a project, and then reciprocated on his own at a later date. But in the islands and outside of the U.S., formal bartering is quite acceptable and, in some countries, the only way to buy.

Some of the more interesting swaps I've heard:

- A chocolate cake made in a frying pan on top of the stove, and the recipe for it, in exchange for a can of hamburgers
- *Playboy* magazines for lobsters and a cruising permit in Costa Rica
- Cigarettes for fresh fish
- A can of spray lacquer for ten green coconuts and a bottle of rum
- In Central America, dime-store trinkets, T-shirts and candy bars for fruit, fish, lobster and water
- Dockage in exchange for watching a small marina for the owner for a day
- English lessons for Spanish lessons
- A day's work on a pineapple plantation for fresh fish and pineapple
- Native musicians playing their instruments and dancing in exchange for a boat tour and dinner
- Refrigeration repair for canned goods and staples
- Artwork for native clothing
- An evening sail, with the island's patriarch at the wheel, for a case of pineapple rum
- Slip rental for ten hours of work per week at the marina
- One night's bar tab and a freshwater shower for tending bar at a Virgin Islands resort
- Six cans of cola and a half-melted bag of ice (value, $16) for minor diesel repairs
- Three homegrown tomatoes for installing software on a computer and training the owner's child in its use

And so on. With bartering, you are only limited by your skills, needs, wants, extra supplies and imagination.

CHAPTER THIRTEEN

WINE, DINE AND PLAY LIKE A KING—ON A PAUPER'S BUDGET

"One cannot think well, love well, sleep well, if one has not dined well."
Virginia Woolf

When you're ready to provision for that first big cruise—whether for two weeks or two years—saving on food, water, beverages and entertainment should be givens. Though many cruisers worry about serious provisioning only when they are headed outside the U.S., having staples and goodies aboard stateside saves on transportation to and from the supermarket, and high prices found in supermarkets in small towns (and even some big ones). Many marinas, not to mention anchorages, are not within walking distance of stores, so it pays to have plenty of staples before you go. You can replenish fresh fruits and vegetables, bread and milk on a day-to-day basis, usually fairly inexpensively. But even on the Intracoastal Waterway in Florida and Georgia, we've gone days without finding a store that could fill all of our needs.

If you are headed to sea, the need to provision is obvious; there are no floating stores around. And in island nations, even the Bahamas, everything is flown in, so the cost is much higher. Add to that duty paid on incoming goods, and $3 a roll for paper towels is the norm. Worse, one of the hardest things to find overseas is good beef, chicken and other meats. Eating fruits and vegetables in some countries can create health problems; the same goes for water. So it's imperative that you stock these items before you go, or find the best places to buy them.

MEATS

Unlike at home where you can store large portions of meats in the freezer for a year or more, sailboats have little freezer space, or none at all. And every cruising sailor knows what happens when you head offshore with a freezer full of steaks and other goodies—the refrigeration is the first thing to go on the blink, and it needs a part you don't have or can't easily get. All the more reason to rely on nonperishable meat sources.

One way is to buy canned meats. Unfortunately, you won't find a huge selection of canned meats in the U.S.. You're pretty much limited to roast beef (hard to find), tuna (everywhere), potted and spiced meats (expensive), Spam (no comment) and maybe canned bacon (many Kmart stores carry it) and chicken (small cans, like tuna, and expensive). Ditto crabmeat and shrimp, but canned salmon is often a good buy. You're better off with roast beef hash and corned beef hash, good old Dinty Moore, and chicken and dumplings when it comes to dinner. But how many days can you eat that stuff?

Next time, try canning your own meats. You can do this at home, but it's time-consuming and may be dangerous if not properly done. Or you can check into a community canning center and spend a day or less canning anything you want safely and cheaply.

Community canning centers were established many years ago to provide farmers and low-income urban and suburban dwellers a way to preserve what they grew. But they are open to anyone, and most are free. Usually, all you pay for is the tin cans, from $.20 to $.30 each, depending on the size. Each canning center may have its own rules and regulations, but here's how one in Jacksonville, Florida, works:

Make an appointment. Bring in meats, vegetables or anything else you want to can. Bring your own paper towels, spices and bouillon. To save time, have everything ready: If you plan to can hamburgers or sausage, have the patties ready; for stew beef, have the meat already cut. Chickens can be brought in whole and washed.

The wonderful people who run the center will help you get started. You'll be assigned a space that includes the use of long stainless steel tables for preparation, an assortment of industrial-size cooking utensils and pots and pans, a stove for browning and simmering broths and a rolling cart for your completed cans.

Estimate how many cans you'll need and what size (No. 10, like vegetables come in, or No. 15, the bigger ones). The cans are washed and set out to dry. Meats such as hamburgers and meatballs should be browned first, easily done in the huge broiler in minutes. Then they are placed into the cans and filled with liquid to within an inch of the top. Beef bouillon is the best choice of liquid for beef; chicken bouillon or water is best for chicken.

For canned chicken pieces, easy to whip into almost any meal and ideal for chicken salad, bring whole washed chickens and put them in an industrial-size pressure cooker, about ten at a time. When done, in about an hour, cool them in front of a fan and debone the chicken. Then fill the cans with the meat and fill with liquid.

Once the cans are ready to go, the canning workers will take them from you. Clean up and you're free to leave. You'll return the next day, or later that afternoon, to pick up your finished products, which will stay fresh a year or more.

I only can meats without sauces because they provide more variety at sea. Canned meatballs can be added to canned spaghetti sauce, stirred into a variety of sauces for hors d'oeuvres, or mixed with other sauces to make main dishes served over rice or noodles, such as sweet and sour meatballs or Swedish meatballs. Hamburgers can be served on buns, as a "steak" or crumbled and used in any recipe that calls for hamburger, such as tacos. Chunks or cubes of beef can also be used in numerous recipes, from stir-fry to soups to stew; the same for the chicken pieces.

One thing to remember is that the canning process takes about an hour and your canned goods are cooked at high pressure. So choose meats that taste good after such treatment. No, the hamburgers aren't great, but after a month or so without one they'll taste wonderful. I've found that chicken and turkey do best under this process, as do the meatballs and inexpensive cuts of roast that you would normally cook for hours to make tender.

The beauty of self-canning, besides the savings, is that you can regulate salt and seasonings for those on special diets. Also, if you are cruising in the hot tropics, the meats are already cooked, so you only have to warm them. That means you'll spend less time in the galley, keep the boat cooler and save on fuel.

You should also can the broth from the chicken that comes from the pressure cooker; it's excellent for soups and gravies, or for cooking rice and pasta for added flavor. Any fat in the cans rises to the top and congeals, so when you open the can, you can skim if off and have virtually fat-free meals.

To find a canning kitchen near you, start with your local department of agriculture, city or county information line, home extension or home economics office. Also ask home economics teachers at high schools. If you can't find one there, try state agencies. Chances are good that somewhere in your area or state you'll find a canning kitchen.

If you can't find one, or don't want to try your hand at canning, there are other ways to buy canned goods inexpensively. Check the yellow pages under Food Products, Wholesale. Tell them about your cruising plans and see if they will be willing to sell you cases of canned goods.

Once you leave the U.S., the variety of canned goods available increases, but the cost may increase as well. Still, if you have little or no refrigeration, canned butter and cream are good choices and go a long way.

Some sailors will argue that cans are heavy and constitute too much weight on board. True, but they can be distributed throughout the boat. Or you can combine canned foods with freeze-dried products and shelf products.

Dried beans, rice and pasta are staples that store well and make for diversified meals. Beans can be made into soups, used as side dishes or added to other soups. Rice and pasta can be fixed a number of ways, hot or cold, by varying the ingredients and spices, creating meals that you won't tire of so easily.

FREEZE-DRIED, DRIED, POWDERED AND DEHYDRATED PRODUCTS

In Utah and California, a number of companies sell freeze-dried meats in cans and other containers. Full meals, such as beef stew and shrimp creole, are available.

Shelf meals, those that need no refrigeration, are available in grocery stores and many sporting goods stores from a number of manufacturers, but many have to be microwaved. They are also expensive.

Powdered foods, such as eggs, milk, juice and cheese are other good provisioning choices.

For staples, military commissaries and wholesalers such as Sam's Club, a Wal-Mart chain found in most U.S. cities, carry bulk packages of rice, flour, sugar and other staples. Some of these staples are actually cheaper to buy overseas.

Freeze-dried onions, bell peppers and chives can be purchased in grocery stores (they're on the spice rack) and added to foods.

Dried fruits, raisins, cranberries, apricots and banana slices store well and are delectable snacks at sea. They're also good to have on hand to perk up salads and baked goods.

OVERSEAS BARGAINS
- Australia, New Zealand—Canned meats and dairy products.
- Caribbean—Canned butter, soft flour, rice, dried beans, canned cream, rum. Some fresh vegetables: tomatoes, squash, breadfruit, coconut.

Fruits: avocado, mango, limes, papaya, bananas, guavas, pineapple, sapodilla, passion fruit.

- Hawaii, Guam—Large variety of U.S. foods at good prices, but higher than what you're accustomed to paying in the U.S.
- South America—Locally brewed beer, fresh fruit and vegetables, fish. Dried beans. Tomatoes, squash, breadfruit, coconut, avocado, mango, limes, papaya, bananas, guavas, sapodilla, passion fruit.

Perma-Pak
40 E. 2430 S., Salt Lake City, UT 84115, (801) 268-3913

Surplus Center
P.O. Box 82209, Lincoln, NE 68501, (402) 474-5167

STOWING FOOD AND BEVERAGES

When it comes to stowing food, less is more, in terms of packaging, regardless of where you sail or cruise. Garbage facilities are nonexistent on most Caribbean islands and, of course, in anchorages. Carrying bags of garbage around for days doesn't make for pleasant cruising. So take less before you leave.

Use plastic containers with tight-sealing lids that can be washed instead of thrown away. For more storage flexibility, buy boxes of plastic bags in various sizes, or invest in a Seal-A-Meal kit, found in most department or discount stores. Empty boxes of mashed potatoes, pasta, rice and other foods into the bags. Then tear off the cooking instructions, usually on the back of the carton, and put it inside the plastic bag. Bags take up less space than boxes and make for more flexible storage.

One river cruiser empties bottles of wine into Seal-A-Meal pouches in carafe-size portions. The bags are kept cool and dry in the bilge! She also finds the bags a good way to seal and store parts, tools and other small items, protecting them from corrosion.

Knowing how to store foods also helps save money, because you can buy in bulk, which usually is cheaper than buying smaller portions. Always compare prices.

- Eggs—Flats of fresh, never-refrigerated eggs will keep for a month or more. Though various methods of keeping them fresh abound (coating with petroleum jelly, etc.), the best method is to keep them turned. Put an extra flat on top, and every few days turn the flats upside down, one at a time. You may have trouble finding such eggs in supermarkets because laws require them to be refrigerated for retail sale (because of salmonella). But if you can locate a chicken farmer, he may provide you with fresh eggs.

• Fruits and vegetables—Store in brown paper bags or newspaper, put them in a dry place and they will keep for weeks. Be sure to check them frequently and throw out or eat those that are beginning to spoil. One bad apple *will* spoil the whole batch. Cabbage keeps well for a month or more; fresh carrots for a few weeks. Potatoes and onions should be kept in a dry, dark place; fresh ones may last for two months or longer. Buy green bananas by the stalk and hang them from the mast to ripen. Ditto bags of oranges, grapefruits and limes. As with eggs, try to find fruits and vegetables that have not been refrigerated, which cuts down on their shelf life.

• Staples—Keep flour, sugar, salt, coffee and tea in tight-fitting plastic containers away from moisture. A few grains of rice in a salt shaker with a tight-fitting lid will help, but at sea, moisture will permeate the salt eventually.

• Pasta should also be stored in plastic containers with tight-fitting lids; the rough edges are apt to cut through the bag.

BEVERAGES

Fresh drinking water is a major concern for most boaters, because boats typically don't have large water tanks, and replenishing supplies in foreign ports can be expensive, not to mention of dubious quality. There are several ways to solve the water dilemma.

Invest in a watermaker, or water purifier. One converts salt water to fresh water, the other filters out bacteria and chemicals in questionable water supplies.

Or rig a rain catcher to a bimini or canvas cover. The catcher should drain into a water holder. A nylon stocking makes a good intermediate filter, and a tablespoon of bleach per one hundred gallons of water serves as a disinfectant; it's the same ratio used by municipal water companies. Use the same ratio in the boat's water tanks.

Fresh water can be secured in Seal-A-Meal bags as well.

In areas where water is scarce, and therefore metered and sold, usually at marinas, some marinas will allow you to fill your water tanks for free if you are filling up with fuel. Ask.

Beer is also expensive in many parts of the world, especially in the Caribbean. Take as much as you think you will need, and when you run out, drink native brews. If you're headed to South America, beer is cheap if you buy local brands. Even stateside, you may travel through "dry" counties where beer cannot be purchased at all, or "blue law" states where alcohol is sold only through licensed stores. That could limit the number of places you can purchase it from. And some states and counties don't allow alcohol to be sold on Sundays.

Some brands of alcohol are actually cheaper to buy outside the U.S., most notably rum in the Caribbean, and port and sherry in Spain. Cruising guides for specific areas may provide you with this kind of information.

One of the best new ideas of the 1990s is powdered and concentrated fruit drinks that don't need refrigeration. You'll find these on grocery store shelves.

PAPER GOODS

Almost anywhere outside the U.S., paper goods such as toilet paper, paper towels and napkins are not available or cost a fortune. Again, take what you think you will need and develop new habits: Use a sponge or dishcloth instead of paper towels. Use washcloths for napkins. Use less of everything paper instead of more.

PRODUCE

Fresh produce is usually readily available in most states and countries, but perhaps not convenient to waterways. You may find good produce in grocery stores, or locally grown produce in country stores and restaurants. Fruit and vegetable stands on highways are good places to look, but you may have to hike to find one.

Again, in the Caribbean, fresh produce sells for a premium; most islands can't grow large quantities because of the sandy soil. But you can take it with you!

Tomatoes, especially cherry tomatoes, as well as parsley and other herbs do quite nicely on a sailboat. Pick a sunny window for herbs and put them in a small hanging basket so they won't tip over in a seaway. Tomatoes can be secured to the stern in full sun. The salt spray doesn't seem to bother them; just be sure they get a drink of fresh water if it doesn't rain. Use a heavy, rich soil that won't dry out as frequently as regular potting soil. When you're dying for fresh veggies, a parsley and tomato salad can be manna from heaven.

South and Central America and other countries of the world all grow produce, and usually it is quite inexpensive. But you must be careful about eating the skin, and about washing it in local water supplies. Again, area cruising guides will help you here.

FREE SEAFOOD—ALL YOU CAN EAT!

If you can catch fish, conch, lobster, clams, oysters, shrimp or other sea delicacies, you can eat for months on the bounty of the sea. Of course, you will grow tired of seafood—honest. One can only eat so much grouper and lobster in the Bahamas before it becomes boring and you begin yearning for that "cheeseburger in paradise," as singer-songwriter Jimmy Buffet accurately describes it.

Most sailors take along a fishing pole, shrimp net, crab trap, oyster glove, spear and lobster bag as essential equipment. Be careful before you start your bounty hunting. Most states and foreign countries require licenses to take stock from the sea, and there may be closed seasons for some seafood. Limits (certain sizes and amounts) are common. And for safety's sake, learn where oyster and clam beds are closed because of contamination, and which species and sizes of fish are subject to ciguatera poisoning.

With this knowledge, you can easily and safely eat from the "land." If you're squeamish about catching and preparing your own seafood, you can always buy from the locals. Shrimp boat crew might sell you some of their catch, as may professional fishermen. Or you might be able to convince a wholesaler to sell you some of its catch.

 TIP

Some states do not require a fishing license if you fish with a cane pole, and most have license waivers for children and seniors.

STOVE-TOP COOKING

Many boats don't have ovens, for various reasons: Some sailors remove them because of the tremendous amount of heat they produce (nice in the winter, but horrible in the summer) or to conserve space. You really can cook wonderful meals on a boat without an oven.

Nearly anything you bake in the oven can be duplicated on top of the stove. The trick is to think of the appliance, frying pan or pressure cooker as the oven.

A 10-inch frying pan with a tight-fitting lid is perfect for baking cakes and cookies. Make the batter using a recipe or prepared mix, preheat the pan and pour in the batter. Cover it with a lid and cook it for about the same time called for in the recipe. Since boat stoves vary widely in the type of fuel (propane burns hotter than alcohol), you will need to monitor the flame and time. A container alcohol stove presents a slight challenge, as the flame is concentrated in one place, the middle of the pan. Just rotate the pan around the flame for even cooking. Or buy a flame tamer or diffuser, devices that, added to such stoves, allow the heat to be evenly distributed. Many cake recipes are for two-layer cakes, and a 10-inch pan will only hold one layer. You can make half a batch, cook the layers one after the other or use two pans.

No boat should be without a pressure cooker or a large, heavy metal pot with a tight-fitting lid. Pressure cookers are best because they cook meats, beans and vegetables in a fraction of the time of conventional pots and pans. That means less time in a hot galley and savings on fuel. Used without the pressure valve so the steam can escape, they also are wonderful bread bakers. The secret to getting a brown crust on all sides is to coat the sides with oil and dust it with corn meal. Yummy fresh breads are always available using this method, though the loaves will always be round unless you use miniature loaf pans that will fit into a pressure cooker. You can stack them two high, but may run into problems if the bread rises substantially during cooking.

You can also use the pressure cooker to bake turkey, ham or roast.

STOVE-TOP RECIPES
FRYING PAN CHOCOLATE CAKE

1½ cups flour	⅓ cup cooking oil
1 cup sugar	½ tablespoon vinegar
3 teaspoons cocoa	1 teaspoon vanilla
1 teaspoon soda	1 cup cold water
½ teaspoon salt	

Mix dry ingredients in an 8-inch frying pan. Make three holes with a spoon in the mixture. Pour oil, vinegar and vanilla into each hole. Pour water over entire mixture and stir until all ingredients are moistened. Put lid on frying pan and cook over low heat for 30 minutes. Leave in pan and frost with icing of choice, if desired.

WHOLE WHEAT BREAD

2½ cups warm water	2 cups whole wheat flour
1 package dry yeast	¼ cup instant dry milk
3 tablespoons butter or	1 teaspoon salt
margarine	4 cups white flour
¼ cup honey	

Dissolve yeast in ¼ cup water. Melt margarine and add honey and remaining water. Add flour, dry milk and salt to the mixture, beating until smooth. Blend in yeast. Mix in flour to make a dough that doesn't cling to the pot. Knead about 10 minutes. Place in a greased bowl and turn. Cover with a towel and let rise in a warm place about 1½ hours, or until doubled in size. Punch down dough and divide into two small loaves or one large one. Cover with a towel and let stand 5 minutes. Shape into loaves and place in loaf pans, or place in pressure cooker greased and dusted with cornmeal. Brush tops with melted butter. Cover and let rise about 1 hour. Bake on low to medium heat for 50 minutes. If using a pressure cooker, remove the pressure valve.

BEER BREAD

3 cups self-rising flour	¼ cup melted butter
1 can warm beer	2 tablespoons honey

Mix flour, beer and honey together. Pour into a greased loaf pan or greased pressure cooker. Pour melted butter over dough. Bake on low heat for one hour. If using pressure cooker, remove pressure valve.

ONE-POT MEALS

CHICKEN WITH YELLOW RICE AND BLACK BEANS

1 bag yellow rice mix (Virgo is the best)	1 can chicken bouillon (or enough water for rice recipe with chicken bouillon cubes added)
2 small cans chicken	1 can black beans

Follow the directions for the rice. When it comes to a boil, add chicken before covering. About 5 minutes before it's done, pour a can of black beans over the top and continue cooking.

CHILI

1 pound hamburger (or 1 can of hamburgers)	1 can chopped tomatoes
	1 can tomato sauce
1 can spicy chile beans	1 package chili mix

Brown meat, if raw, in a large pot. Pour contents of all cans into pot, bring to a boil and simmer for 10 to 15 minutes.

ROAST TURKEY IN A POT

1 six to eight pound turkey

Wash turkey and place in pressure cooker, breast side up. Add ½ cup water. Cook with pressure valve off over low heat for time indicated on turkey bag (about 2 hours).

BOAT COOKBOOKS

Pierce, Charles. *365 Ways to Cook Fish and Shellfish*. New York: HarperCollins, 1993.

Sass, Lorna J. *Cooking Under Pressure*. New York: Morrow, 1989.

FLOWERS AND PLANTS

For some, sailing without greenery around may be hard to bear. Elizabeth Rush found a solution for those who love plants: She purchased a gold-dust aucuba, a small plant with green, glossy leaves and gold splotches, from Kmart for $1.59. It is drought resistant, doesn't need sun and has survived on her boat for seven years, going without attention for weeks at a time. She says the plant isn't always labeled by its botanical name, so look for it with a tag that says "tropical foliage."

For the cockpit, aloe, which is good for burns and bites (but some people are allergic to it), makes a pretty plant and is hardy. Another good choice is portulaca, or moss rose, a succulent with tiny green leaves and huge multi-colored flowers. I've had the same plant on my boat for four years. It does well surviving only on dew and rainwater, and comes back year after year.

Herbs grown in small pots also do well on boats and in a saltwater environment. Chives, oregano, mint, parsley and rosemary are good choices. Grow them from seed in small pots and then transfer them to larger pots as needed. Be careful not to let the garden outgrow the boat.

Neumeyer, Ken. *Sailing the Farm*. Berkeley: Ten Speed Press, 1981.

FUN AND GAMES—ONBOARD AND ANCHORAGE ENTERTAINMENT AT A FRACTION OF THE COST OF GOING ASHORE

Entertaining on board is always cheaper than going ashore: You merely have to look for creative ways to do it. On a small boat, or even a big one, having friends over can be tough because of space limitations; more than four is usually a crowd. Constant improvisers, sailors have found ways to have fun and entertain on a budget and in a small space.

When it comes to dining, covered dishes (everyone brings something) go a long way toward helping out the chef with a small stove in a cramped space. And it spreads the cost of dinner over several people instead of just one. Plus, if every guest brings part of the meal, you'll save on cooking fuel, too.

Grilling on a propane or charcoal stove in the cockpit affords more seating room for guests and less worry for the chef: It means one less thing to prepare.

 TIP
Cut a roll of paper towels in half to make two small rolls and save money. The sheets are big enough for most jobs.

Other fun, inexpensive ways to "eat out," especially with a group of friends: Take a picnic lunch to an island or state park. You can take sandwiches, cook out on a grill on the beach (watch the sand) or use the park grills.

Have a progressive dinner in the anchorage, going by dinghy to each person's boat for a different course, or serve heavy hors d'ouevres at each boat, handing food down to guests in a dinghy.

Form a daisy ring of dinghies and pass food from tender to tender (paper plates aren't a good idea here; they tend to fold upon passing) or, better yet, form a raft-up of sailboats. Each boat puts a treat on the cockpit table, and guests go from boat to boat, visiting and dining as they go.

Elegant meals are no more difficult to prepare on a boat than at home—and definitely cheaper than eating out. Lobster, shrimp and fish with butter and lemon sprinkled with paprika; a tossed salad or cole slaw; and a pasta are easy-to-do but elegant meals. Keep a good selection of packaged sauce mixes that require milk or water to make, and use them for such occasions. Hollandaise sauce on asparagus is a special, elegant treat; a can of artichoke hearts added to a salad or pasta dresses up a plain meal.

TIP

One tablespoon of bleach to one hundred gallons of water purifies the water, but doesn't leave a taste or smell of the bleach.

For groups, games that can be played without a table are important. Sitting on a boat all day, or even swimming and exploring, can become tiresome. So when you need some time away with no costs involved, turn to games. Some fun ones that you may remember from your childhood: charades, twenty questions and I Spy. Or simply read the cards from trivia games and keep score by counting the number of right answers. Forming teams is fun, as is pairing couples.

Movie rentals can add up, too, as do trips to the theater—assuming you can find one. But boats equipped with generators or inverters can power a small television with a built-in VCR and a handful of video tapes for a "night at the movies." Make popcorn and sit back and enjoy the show. Our boat was a hit in the Bahamas a few years back, before the stores there started renting videos, when we had a "drive-in movie night." Guests from other boats in the anchorage came in their dinghies, we set the VCR in the cockpit and everyone got to see the show. This also works well at a marina. Put the television set on deck and let everyone bring lawn chairs to set up on the dock.

 TIP

Problems with cockroaches? Sprinkle boric acid around and they'll soon disappear.

During daylight hours, when you may be tempted to shop (and spend money) or seek out a restaurant or bar for companionship (more money), there are endless things to do. But if you want to organize some outdoor games, try cruiser beach volleyball (with a stick in the sand for a net), dinghy races around the anchorage (be careful of your wake) or knot-tying contests, a good way to learn or reinforce your skills.

Three-legged races, sack races and other games from childhood are as fun for adults as they are for children.

Search for green coconuts and make coconut rum punch like the natives do; bring something to strain it with.

CHAPTER FOURTEEN

AWAY FROM THE MADDENING CROWDS

"The happiest hour a sailor sees
Is when he's down
At an inland town
With his Nancy on his knees, yo ho!
And his arm around her waist!"

    W.S. Gilbert, The Mikado

Whether you sail close to home or to faraway ports, popular anchorages and marinas are always crowded during the area's season, usually warm months in the States and cool months in the Caribbean, though that's not always the rule. Some places are year-round destinations because of the climate, or hold a particular attraction, including festivals, during colder months for a number of reasons.

But every sailor knows one particular harbor, anchorage, island or marina that is off the beaten path. Such places are found in every state, in every island nation and in all corners of the world.

Your search may include seeking free or low-cost marinas—and, yes, they are out there. When you're cruising for weeks and months at a time, saving money is the name of the game. Most anchorages are free, but access to land may not be. You'll frequently be in search of supplies, water, fuel, a Laundromat and maybe even showers. To reach them, you may have to pay a dinghy dockage fee, which often includes use of a facility's showers, dumpster and other amenities. There are many ways to reach land and services without spending a fortune.

Your search may also include the tranquility of an island paradise—a sun-drenched beach with sand so fine that it squeaks beneath your feet—or a wooded isle, crisp, cool, green and inviting, with rocks to explore. Such places can still be found worldwide.

FREE DOCKAGE

As mentioned, small towns, states and cities may offer free dockage to transient sailors. But so do some restaurants and retail stores that are on the water. A Burger King restaurant in Palatka, Florida, on the St. Johns River, has a long dock for patrons. Most waterway restaurants will let you tie up at least for a meal, and some will let you stay overnight. Be sure to ask. State parks often have docks, but may restrict dockage to daylight hours. Find these by asking fellow cruisers or by reading area cruising guides.

If you are unable to access a free dock with your sailboat, try anchoring and tying up your dinghy. Some of the resources listed above may not have a dock or the dock may be in shallow water. But they may allow a free dinghy tie-up for the day, which will enable you to tend to shopping, laundry and other needs. Always lock your dinghy. Most people are honest but, as we all know, some are not.

POPULAR CRUISING GUIDES

Calder, Nigel. *The Cruising Guide to the Northwest Caribbean: The Yucatan Coast of Mexico, Belize, Guatemala, Honduras and the Bay Islands.* New York: McGraw-Hill, 1991.

Calhoun, Bruce and Dave Calhoun. *Cruising the San Juan Islands.* Bellevue, WA: Weatherly Press, 1991.

Charles, Simon. *Cruising Guide to Cuba.* Donedin, FL: Cruising Guide, 1994.

Doyle, Chris. *Cruising Guide to the Leeward Islands: Complete Guide for Yachtsmen, Divers.* Donedin, FL: Cruising Guide, 1993.

Doyle, Chris. *Sailor's Guide to the Windward Islands.* Donedin, FL: Cruising Guide, 1992.

Fields, Meredith, ed. *Yachtsman's Guide to the Bahamas.* Atlantic Highlands, NJ: Tropic Isle Publishers, 1990.

Kiurski, Gayle. *The Other Way South (Michigan to Mobile).* Bonita Springs, FL: Tag Press, 1995.

Marian, Thomas and W.J. Rumsey. *A Cruising Guide to the Tennessee River, Tenn-Tom Waterway and Lower Tombigbee River.* Camden, ME: International Marine, 1995.

Papy, Captain Frank. *Cruising Guide to the Florida Keys*. Ridgeland, SC: F. Papy Cruising Guide, 1988.

Scott, Simon and Nancy Scott. *Cruising Guide to the Virgin Islands*. Donedin, FL: Cruising Guide, 1994.

Smith, Robert D. and Barbara A.M. Smith. *Intracoastal Waterway Facilities Guide*. Winter Park, CO: Paradox Publishing, 1994.

Smyth, Gina. *Cruising the Okeechobee Waterway*. P.O. Box 21586, Fort Lauderdale, FL 33335, (305) 462-8151.

Stone, William and Anne Hays. *A Cruising Guide to the Caribbean: Including the North Coast of South America, Central America and Yucatan*. Dobbs Ferry, NY: Sheridan, 1993.

Van Sant, Bruce. *The Gentleman's Guide to Passage South*. Fort Lauderdale: B. Van Sant, 1989.

Young, Claiborne S. *Cruising Guide to Coastal North Carolina*. Winston-Salem, NC: Blair, 1994.

Young, Claiborne S. *Cruising Guide to Coastal South Carolina and Georgia*. Winston-Salem, NC: Blair, 1993.

Young, Claiborne S. *Cruising Guide to Eastern Florida*. Kailua Kona, HI: Pelican, 1995.

Young, Claiborne S. *Cruising Guide to the Northern Gulf Coast: Florida, Alabama, Mississippi, Louisiana*. Kailua Kona, HI: Pelican, 1995.

Young, Claiborne S. *Cruising Guide to Western Florida*. Kailua Kona, HI: Pelican, 1995.

TRANSPORTATION

Getting from the boat to the dinghy to land is one thing. Getting around on land is another. You can call a taxi (usually expensive) or ride a local bus if you're near a bus line. Riding a bus is a great way to see a foreign country and take in the culture and people. It's usually the most inexpensive way to see the country. The buses may be piled high with adults and children in colorful clothing, luggage and goods in sacks and bags, and sometimes even livestock and produce on its way to and from the market. Stateside, a bus may take you swiftly to a giant mall, or to a tiny town or village. Sometimes, it's fun just to see where the bus goes, but make sure it comes back to where you boarded it—the same day!

A number of small towns, especially those in tourist areas, have a bus or shuttle that stops at tourist sites and shopping malls. Some are free, some charge only a dollar, and on most you may get on and off as often as you wish.

Friendly townsfolk and fellow land-bound sailors often will offer rides; again, especially in small communities. In some towns, residents come to the docks each night to look at the boats that have arrived. They may offer rides or extend invitations to dinner. At marinas, liveaboard sailors who are land-bound and working, usually have a car and often offer to take you where you need to go.

Take a bicycle. Many cruisers take fold-up bikes (purchased from specialty electronics, bicycle or marine stores or catalogs) for healthy, cheap transportation. Be aware that some states have laws requiring the use of helmets, lights at night, and reflectors, and some countries and island nations may forbid them or require a special certificate. Nonfolding bikes also work well on larger boats where there is adequate space to store them and where they are protected from salt spray.

Grocery stores, marine stores, hardware stores and restaurants often provide a one-way or round-trip ride to or from their establishments. If you're staying at a marina, employees usually know of such services, or the retailer will post a notice on the marina's bulletin board. Sometimes you may find your way to the store, and will be offered a ride back.

DINING OUT

Eating out is expensive when you're cruising on a budget, but again, it's not out of the question. Many restaurants serve dinner-size meals at lunch at prices 30 to 50 percent less than for the same meal at dinner. Lunch hours are usually posted, so if lunch specials end at 4 P.M., eat dinner early on a lunch budget. Or if lunch ends at 2 P.M., order a hearty lunch, have the restaurant wrap up the leftovers and then serve them for dinner. Take advantage of two-for-one specials, and check local free newspapers for coupons.

If you're near a college or university, check to see if the cafeteria allows "outsiders." Often they serve good food at budget prices: Some are "all you can eat" cafeterias, some serve boardinghouse style.

Excellent, inexpensive meals can often be found in hospital cafeterias. Most of these are open to the public.

LAND-BASED ENTERTAINMENT

For the price, you can't beat national, state, city and county parks. Most cost under $5 per adult (many are free) and provide a wealth of outdoor and cultural information. Typically, they have bathroom facilities, fishing and swimming areas with lifeguards, boat ramps and docks. Some have restaurants and museums; others are on historic sites.

Museums are also a good way to spend a day or half day at a small cost or for free. You'll find them in most cities and states, as well as overseas. Even tiny Hope Town in the Abacos area of the Bahamas has a wonderful museum with artifacts of the Arawak Indians from a dig near the museum. There are maritime, art, music, car and sport museums throughout the world; the list is endless.

Local concerts, fairs, waterfront festivals, high school and college plays and recitals are good sources of entertainment. Many are free, or the admission charge is nominal. Plus, it's a good way to meet people who live in the area and to sample local fare.

One of the finest meals I ate in the Bahamas was at an inn hosting the interisland dart-throwing competition. Besides meeting some wonderful people, the buffet spread of native meats, fish and vegetables, cooked over outdoor grills, was remarkable. The price was $8 per person for all you cared to eat. Check with chambers of commerce, visitors' bureaus and state and federal parks for a list of festivities, attractions and museums in the areas you intend to cruise.

TOWNS AND ANCHORAGES— SAILOR'S PICKS

To list every wonderful town, anchorage and marina would be impossible, but the following are some tried and true places that sailors have mentioned over and over. They are listed for destinations that sailors typically cruise to, yet many are out-of-the-way spots along the route.

BAHAMAS
ABACOS, REGATTA TIME IN ABACO
July 3 through July 10
(305) 946-3467

Racing and sailing around islands, great parties, free food and beverages.

CHEROKEE SOUND
Dicey entrance around reef, but small, seldom-visited fishing and boatbuilding town. Watch natives pull in 16-foot tiger sharks in small boats with large outboards. Whole village comes out to watch the men cut up the sharks. Shops, bakery and garbage facility.

FROZEN ALDER CAY, BERRY ISLANDS
Breathtaking island and anchorage in crystal clear deep-turquoise water. White sandy beaches full of palm trees. Reefs inside. No facilities and few visitors.

GEORGE TOWN, EXUMA
The meeting place for cruising sailors. They come; they stay.

LITTLE HARBOUR (JOHNSTON'S ISLAND)
Home of the late artist, Randolph Johnston, foundry, pub, beach, old light-house, walk to beautiful shallow reef, multitude of green turtles. Robinson's Bight nearby teems with fish, lobster, conch and blue holes.

SANDY POINT
Small fishing village of about four hundred people. Anchor behind island; local knowledge only to get into sheltered water. Very friendly natives, shops, grocery, lots of conch, fish and nearby reefs. Few visitors.

STANIEL CAY, EXUMA
Paradise, crystal clear water. James Bond movie filmed here. Shops, marina, anchorage and limited supplies.

BRITISH VIRGIN ISLANDS
CANE GARDEN BAY
Tour Callwood Rum Distillery for $1 per person.

GREAT HARBOR, FOXY'S
One of best bars in the Caribbean.

GULF
BROADWATER BEACH, MISSISSIPPI
Marina. Historic homes in town, most notably Jefferson Davis's, president of the Confederacy, in Beauvoir. Short ride to historic district. Restaurants, shops and facilities.

CITY OF PORT LAVACA, TEXAS
(512) 552-2615

City-run marina in small town of about 11,000 people. Dockage $2 per foot per month, or $5 a day. Hurricane hole, groceries, hardware and propane nearby. Twenty-five miles south of Victoria and twenty miles from Gulf of Mexico.

INGRAM BAYOU, ALABAMA
Pristine anchorage with good protection. Forested coastline is great for exploring.

LAKE PONTCHARTRAIN, LOUISIANA
Small towns, marinas and anchorages. Cajun restaurants.

NORTHEAST
BANNISTER'S WHARF, NEWPORT, RHODE ISLAND
A number of marinas adjacent to specialty shops. Near Newport. Fishing boat fleet nearby. Several good restaurants, all within walking distance. Newport is a bustling waterfront town with historic district. Museums nearby.

BAY OF FUNDY, NOVA SCOTIA
Not for fainthearted because of extreme tides (fifty feet plus), currents and rips, but rare beauty, friendly people and quaint villages.

BULLOCK COVE, BARRINGTON, RHODE ISLAND
Marinas, small village of Bay Springs, park, beaches and picnicking. Small restaurants and Laundromat.

CAPE CHARLES (EASTERN SHORE OF VIRGINIA)
No anchorage, but you can stay at the town dock for about $15 a day or $50 a week. Easy walk to facilities; lots of friendly people.

CHESAPEAKE BAY (THE POTOMAC RIVER DIVIDES MARYLAND AND VIRGINIA)

DEAL ISLAND, MARYLAND (HARBOR AT CHANCE, EASTERN SHORE)
No facilities, but you can dinghy ashore and ask permission to watch the crab pickers at the seafood factory. They sit at long tables, their fingers flying as they pick the meat from the crabs. Often they will break out in song.

ESSEX, CONNECTICUT
Eighteenth Century Village, known as "Camelot on the Connecticut River." Shops, grocery stores, bookstores and many marinas. All wants and needs filled here.

HADLEY HARBOR, NAUSHON, MASSACHUSETTS
Protected, unspoiled island. Good anchorage.

HAMPTON, VIRGINIA (INTRACOASTAL WATERWAY)
Historic town, often quite crowded. Visitor's center is on the water and offers free dinghy dockage. City bus runs along the waterfront for visits to shops.

HORSESHOE BEND (POTOMAC RIVER TO CHESAPEAKE BAY, NORTH BANK, ST. MARY'S RIVER)

Anchor and row ashore. Walk up bank to St. Mary's College, a historical college with a student cafeteria that serves the public. All you can eat meals for $3.50.

JAMESTOWN ISLAND, VIRGINIA (WESTERN SHORE OF THE JAMES RIVER)

Water in this anchorage is deep and swift; anchor in settled weather. From the waterfront, you can see the huge statue of Captain John Smith. Circumnavigate the island by dinghy, or tie up to a tree and walk around the settlement; admission to the settlement is free. Visit Wanda's lunch counter. You'll find eight barstools and one main course a day, all you can eat for about $4. Tomatoes are homegrown.

MYSTIC SEAPORT, CONNECTICUT

The famous New England museum and seaport draw thousands of sailors. Tall ships, quaint shops, good seafood restaurants and marinas.

ONANCOCK, VIRGINIA (EASTERN SHORE ANCHORAGE)

Tie up your dinghy at the public docks free. Several local restaurants, coffee shops, bakery and a distant grocery store. A friendly local may offer you a ride.

OXFORD, MARYLAND (EASTERN SHORE)

Can be a rough anchorage in bad weather, but in good weather you can anchor off the waterfront and leave your dinghy at the beach. A short walk takes you to a small, limited grocery store where you can buy ice cream, and to a public park. There are several good seafood restaurants.

PENOBSCOT BAY, MAINE

Dozens of small towns, islands and coves. Lobster country. Amenities, marinas and various towns. Hundreds of anchorages.

SOLOMON'S ISLAND TO HOLIDAY INN ANCHORAGE (WESTERN SHORE OF CHESAPEAKE BAY, PATUXENT RIVER TO BACK CREEK)

You can tie up your dinghy for $1 a day. Walk two blocks to supermarket and stores. Grocery store will drive you back to the boat. Maritime museum $3, but you can spend the day.

SPA CREEK, ANNAPOLIS, MARYLAND

Anchor out and take the dinghy to the end of any street, where you can tie it up and walk a short distance to downtown Annapolis's historic district, shops and bus line. From there you can get to the monorail that will whisk you to Washington, DC. Also, the Amish Farmer's Market where the Amish go on Fridays, Saturdays and Sundays to sell their produce.

TANGIER ISLAND, MARYLAND, NEAR CRISFIELD

Discovered by Captain John Smith. People who live on the island are descendants of the original settlers. There are no cars on the island and no deep-water docks, but you can anchor and tie up your dinghy for $8 at a small boat dock owned by Milton Parks. The price includes water and showers. Take the mail boat to the mainland along with the locals.

TOMS RIVER, NEW JERSEY

Historic lighthouse, many marinas, lots of lobster restaurants, shopping and facilities.

URBANA, VIRGINIA (RAPPAHANNOCK RIVER, WEST SHORE TO URBANA CREEK ANCHOR AND ROW ASHORE)

Free landing, but ask permission. Walk up the hill to a very small, old historic town. City fathers meet in coffee shop each morning. Laundromat and supermarket.

VIRGINIA, NORTHERNMOST REACHES OF POTOMAC RIVER (AS FAR AS A SAILBOAT CAN GO BEFORE REACHING A LOW BRIDGE)

Anchor out, dinghy ashore. There's one marina and one yacht club where you can keep your dinghy and use the showers and Laundromat for $5 a night. It's a short walk to the nation's capital and the Washington Monument. Excellent transportation via monorail and buses.

WEST POINT, VIRGINIA (THE WEST SHORE OF THE YORK RIVER)

Very old, small town where you can anchor and tie up the dinghy at a waterfront seafood restaurant. There's a local coffee shop owned by a former jockey, who serves Greek fare along with Southern traditional fare. Library and many historical homes.

NORTHWEST

BLAKE ISLAND, WASHINGTON (450-ACRE STATE PARK ISLAND IN PUGET SOUND)

Accessible only by boat. Small dock, anchorage.

CALIFORNIA DELTA, ANDRUS ISLAND
Marinas, shops, nearby creeks, islands and anchorages for exploring.

OAKLAND ESTUARY, CALIFORNIA
Marinas and waterside restaurants with docks. Alameda side has Victorian homes. Channel between Oakland and Alameda.

PENDER ISLANDS, CANADA
Many anchorages and harbors. Restaurants and facilities.

ROCHE HARBOR, SAN JUAN ISLAND
Restaurants, shops and sheltered harbor.

VICTORIA, VANCOUVER, BRITISH COLUMBIA
Excellent harbor, Old World atmosphere in a modern city. Shops, restaurants, parks and gardens.

WEST SOUND, ORCAS ISLAND, SAN JUAN ISLANDS
Good harbor, shops and restaurants.

SOUTHEAST
BANANA RIVER, FLORIDA (OFF THE INTRACOASTAL WATERWAY PAST TITUSVILLE).
Anchor and watch the space shuttle. No facilities; marina accessed via lock.

CUMBERLAND ISLAND, FLORIDA (INTRACOASTAL WATERWAY BETWEEN GEORGIA AND FLORIDA STATE LINE)
Protected island owned by federal park service, former playground of Carnegies. Short sail to historic St. Mary's, Georgia, and Fernandina Beach, Florida, a Victorian seaport town.

DISMAL SWAMP CANAL (BETWEEN VIRGINIA AND NORTH CAROLINA)
North Carolina has a visitor's center where Highway 17 parallels the canal, a project conceived by George Washington. Free overnight dockage for a day or two. No facilities. Visitor's center has a garden where native summer vegetables, including peanuts, are grown. Look, don't pick.

EAU GALLIE, FLORIDA
Good anchorage off a larger-than-life dragon, which guards the point. Dinghy to marina for access to fuel, ice and short walk to shops, malls and hardware stores.

ELIZABETH CITY, NORTH CAROLINA
Offers free dockage for forty-eight hours. Friendly locals often will take you into town. Restaurants will pick you up and bring you back for free. A group called the Rose Buddies greets new arrivals in the afternoon and provides a wine and cheese party if there are three or more newly arrived boats. Historic town with a good used book store, supermarket and Laundromat.

EVERGLADES CITY, FLORIDA
Another entrance to Everglades National Park. No anchorage, but several marinas. Shops and grocery; small quaint town swarms with tourists in winter, laid back in summer. Historic Rod & Gun Club open to public.

FLAMINGO, FLORIDA
One entrance to Everglades National Park. Marina and lodge, very busy during winter. Walking and canoe trails. Limited groceries and ice.

JACKSONVILLE, FLORIDA, ORTEGA RIVER
(TRIBUTARY OF ST. JOHNS RIVER)
Good, sheltered anchorage and many marinas. Marine stores, restaurants, grocery store, mall and Laundromat within walking distance.

KEY BISCAYNE, FLORIDA
Good anchorages along key at national park. Cape Florida lighthouse at tip of island; picnicking, swimming and exploring.

LABELLE, FLORIDA, OKEECHOBEE WATERWAY.
Free dockage for three nights. Small, friendly town. Locals come to greet boaters after work. Honey capital of Florida; buy jars of different types in nearby stores. Restaurants. Annual Swamp Cabbage festival.

MOREHEAD CITY, NORTH CAROLINA
Tony's Sanitary Restaurant offers free dockage with meal.

PALATKA, FLORIDA (ST. JOHNS RIVER)
Free dockage at city dock, limited power and water. Historic small town, restaurants and shops. Ravines State Park nearby.

PEANUT ISLAND, FLORIDA (WEST PALM BEACH)
Anchoring around island. Good access on northern side to shops, stores,

grocery, ice cream, restaurants. Popular as a jump-off spot for the Bahamas via Lake Worth Inlet.

ST. AUGUSTINE, FLORIDA
Large anchorage and many marinas, oldest city in U.S. Fort, museums, historic buildings, shops, restaurants, grocery and city marina.

As mentioned, these are just a sampling of favorite cruising spots. As you begin to sample what your area has to offer, you'll find that one particular harbor few know about—an enchanted place where you feel all the cares and worries of the world fade away.

If you have trouble finding one of your own, ask around; nearly every sailor has a favorite spot. That place may be desolate, or populated but quaint. It may be an island hideaway or a spot on a placid river. It may be a bustling harbor where fun abounds on shore, or a tiny swimming hole with great shore-based facilities.

It has to do with choices. As you have learned from this book, sailors are individuals whose needs and wants differ greatly. One man's paradise is another man's bane. Some sailors like to get to the destination as quickly as possible and then relax. Others consider the trip part of the adventure.

When it comes to the boat itself, few sailors can agree on which is best. This decision, of course, is as individual as the person or people selecting the boat, his or their needs, budgets and desires. There's always a tradeoff. And many prefer to not own a boat, relying on friends, acquaintances and charters to fill their sailing needs.

That's why sailing is such a versatile sport. It can—and does—meet the needs of all individuals, from pauper to millionaire.

As you begin or continue your journey into sailing, you too will find nifty and thrifty ways to sail. Sailing can be done on a budget.

I wish you fair winds, following seas, personal adventures and a lifetime of fun and enjoyment.

INDEX